Praying wi

Praying with Jesus

What the Gospels Tell Us about How to Pray

George Martin

Loyola Press
Chicago

Loyola Press

3441 North Ashland Avenue
Chicago, Illinois 60657

Previous versions of this book were published under the titles *To Pray as Jesus* (Servant Books, 1978) and *Praying with Jesus* (Liguori, 1989).

The Scripture quotations contained herein are from the New Revised Standard Version Bible: Catholic Edition copyright © 1993 and 1989 by the Division of Christian Education of the National Council of the Churches of Christ in the U.S.A. Used by permission. All rights reserved.

Interior design by Jennifer Mindel

Library of Congress Cataloging-in-Publication Data
Martin, George, 1939–

   Praying with Jesus : what the Gospels tell us about how to pray / George Martin.

      p. cm.

   Originally published: Liguori, Mo. : Liguori Publications, c1989.

   ISBN 0-8294-1476-2

   1. Jesus Christ—Prayers. 2. Prayer—Christianity. I. Title.

   BV229 .M28 2000

   248.3'2—dc21   99-049224

Printed in the United States of America
00 01 02 03 04 / 10 9 8 7 6 5 4 3 2 1

For Frank and Julie,
as a prayer

CONTENTS

Praying as Jesus Prayed

Praying is not an obligation imposed on us by God, any more than God commands us, "Thou shalt breathe." Our need to pray arises because we are humans and God is God. The more clearly we recognize who we are and who God is, the more urgent it becomes for us to communicate with the one who holds us in existence.

We may experience our need to pray in a variety of ways. Often we cry out for help or rescue from difficulties: "Lord, have mercy" may be the common denominator of our cries. Sometimes our hearts are filled with gratitude, and our prayers are thanksgiving for what we have received. Sometimes we realize our sinfulness and come before the only one who can both forgive and mend us. Sometimes, perhaps less often for many of us, we are moved to praise and adoration in acknowledgment that God is indeed God. And at times our prayer is an anguished "Why? Why has this befallen me or those I love?"

All of these prayers are expressions of our fundamental need to communicate with God. If God is God, and if our fragile lives are in his hands, then we cannot settle for silence. If God had a post office box or an E-mail address, we might write him. Instead, our spoken or thought words must do, in the faith that he knows our hearts.

Yet even with a faith that God hears, and even with our felt need to communicate with God, prayer does not come easily for many of us. We try to enter into the presence of God but end up in what Frank Sheed aptly termed a "pious coma." Our minds are filled with distractions, a constant loud static that drowns out communication with God. We blame ourselves for not being very good at prayer—and we are probably right.

Our ineptness at prayer should not surprise us: we are finite and sinful creatures trying to communicate with the one in whom "we live and move and have our being" (Acts 17:28). The closer we try to come to God, the more apparent becomes the disparity between Creator and creature. "No one has ever seen God" (John 1:18); all our attempts to visualize God fall infinitely short. Nor are we able to enter God's mind and think his thoughts. "My thoughts are not your thoughts, nor are your ways my ways, says the LORD. For as the heavens are higher than the earth, so are my ways higher than your ways and my thoughts than your thoughts" (Isaiah 55:8–9). As distant as the farthest galaxy is from the earth, even more distant is the one who created galaxies and planets and space and time. It would have been easier for an amoeba to have had a stimulating exchange of ideas with Einstein than it is for us to bridge the gap that separates creature from Creator.

God had mercy on us in our lowliness, and he bridged the gap himself. God spoke "in many and various ways" (Hebrews 1:1) to the descendants of Abraham, revealing himself, inviting men and women to come to know him, inviting them into prayer. And in the fullness of time God sent his Son as the definitive bridge between heaven and earth, between himself and us. Jesus Christ, fully human and fully divine, enables humanity to take on divinity. Jesus allows us to speak to the God whom we cannot see, the God whose thoughts are beyond our thoughts.

Although divine, as a human being Jesus shared with us a need to pray. The Gospels show that Jesus was a man of prayer. His disciples noticed this and asked him, "Lord, teach us to pray"

(Luke 11:1). And he did. His instructions regarding prayer, his parables about prayer, and above all his own example in praying have much to teach us about the way we should pray.

That is what this book is about: looking at the example set by Jesus when he prayed and listening to his words of instruction about prayer.

1

Jesus Prayed to His Father

He was praying in a certain place, and after he had finished, one of his disciples said to him, "Lord, teach us to pray, as John taught his disciples."

Luke 11:1

Had the disciples never prayed before? Were they so ignorant of prayer that they had to ask Jesus for beginner's instructions? This seems doubtful.

We must presume that the disciples were at least ordinarily devout Jews, formed in the rich heritage of Jewish prayers and blessings. They had the temple as their house of prayer, with its highly developed rituals of sacrifice. They had the book of Psalms as their hymnal, with its songs of praise and repentance, jubilation and lament. They had the Sabbath observance and the annual feasts and celebrations of Judaism. They had their morning prayers and evening prayers and blessings. Prayer was ingrained in the life and culture of Jesus' disciples in a way that most modern men and women will never experience.

Yet they came to Jesus and asked him to teach them to pray. What were they asking for? Did they simply want to have a distinctive style of prayer, something that would mark them as disciples of Jesus? John the Baptizer apparently taught his followers to pray in a way that was unique to them (see Luke 5:33); the followers of Jesus could have been asking for a style of prayer as a sign of their identity. However, the setting in which they asked Jesus to teach them to pray suggests that they had something more in mind.

Jesus often prayed in the presence of his disciples: "Once when Jesus was praying alone, with only the disciples near him, he asked them, 'Who do the crowds say that I am?'" (Luke 9:18). It was in a similar setting that the disciples asked Jesus to teach them to pray: Jesus "was praying in a certain place, and after he had finished, one of his disciples said to him, 'Lord, teach us to pray'" (Luke 11:1). The disciples had watched Jesus pray and had observed that there was something different about his prayer—different from their traditions, different from the way that they prayed. They wanted to learn this new way of prayer; they wanted to pray as Jesus prayed.

Father

What had the disciples observed when they watched Jesus at prayer? What was different about his prayers?

The most noteworthy characteristic of Jesus' prayers is that he addressed God as "Father." This is the clear evidence of the Gospels, and this was undoubtedly the aspect of his prayer that most astonished and impressed his followers. To us today, there may be nothing very startling about Jesus' praying to God as his Father. To the first-century contemporaries of Jesus, however, such a form of address must have seemed startling. Little in Jewish tradition prepared them for such boldness.

The fatherhood of God is mentioned in the Old Testament, but it is hardly a major theme. Psalm 103 proclaims, "As a father has compassion for his children, so the LORD has compassion for those who fear him" (verse 13). God spoke to his people through the prophet Jeremiah: "I thought you would call me, My Father, and would not turn from following me" (Jeremiah 3:19). Yet the passages in the Old Testament that call God "Father" are relatively few.

Jesus, however, characteristically prayed to God as his Father and spoke of him as his Father. The Gospels contain about 170 occurrences of Jesus' praying to God as his Father or referring to him as his Father; most of these are found in the Gospel of John, which highlights Jesus' relationship to God as his Father. Except for the time he prayed some words from the psalms from the cross, every prayer of Jesus recorded in the Gospels is addressed to God as Father. For example, when Jesus prayed before raising Lazarus from the dead, he prayed, "Father, I thank you for having heard me" (John 11:41).

My Father

Not only did Jesus address and speak of God as Father—he referred to him as "my Father." The Old Testament references to the fatherhood of God generally spoke of God as the Father of the chosen people. Jesus, in contrast, spoke of and prayed to God as his own particular Father. This went well beyond what Jewish piety allowed. To the devout Jew, the idea of referring to God as one's Father must have seemed utterly presumptuous, almost blasphemous.

Yet Jesus prayed to God as his own Father and did so with ease and confidence:

> At that same hour Jesus rejoiced in the Holy Spirit and said, "I thank you, Father, Lord of heaven and earth, because you have hidden these things from the wise and the intelligent and have revealed them to infants; yes, Father, for such was your gracious will. All things have been handed over to me by my Father; and no one knows who the Son is except the Father, or who the Father is except the Son and anyone to whom the Son chooses to reveal him." (Luke 10:21–22)

This was the type of bold and intimate prayer that Jesus' disciples observed. This was the type of prayer, unprecedented in Jewish tradition, that set Jesus apart from everyone else.

Abba, Father

Jesus used the Aramaic word *abba* in addressing God as his Father. Aramaic was the language spoken by Jews living in Palestine at the time of Jesus and hence was Jesus' native tongue. The four

Gospels, written in Greek, preserve for us only a few of the Aramaic words spoken by Jesus. *Abba* is one of them: "Abba, Father, for you all things are possible" (Mark 14:36).

Abba is an informal and colloquial word for *father*. *Abba* is the word that children would use in speaking to their father; it is also the word that they would continue to use in addressing their father after they had grown up and had children of their own. There is no perfect English equivalent for the word *abba*. *Father* is too formal, and *Daddy* is too informal. Perhaps *Dad* comes closest. *Abba* is not baby talk or slang. *Abba* is an intimate, yet respectful, form of address, with a ring of affection.

Jesus probably called Joseph "Abba" from the time he learned to talk until Joseph died. There would have been nothing strange about that. But in his prayers, Jesus also addressed God as "Abba." That was indeed striking and distinctive, something not done by others. While Jesus' prayers were deeply respectful and reverential, they addressed God in very familiar and affectionate terms. Jesus prayed to God not as a distant Father but as a close and loving Abba. Jesus spoke to his heavenly Father with the same intimacy that children have in speaking with their earthly father.

That was what was most remarkable about Jesus' prayers, and that was what Jesus' disciples could not fail to notice when they heard him pray.

The Son of God

If Jesus could speak to God as his Abba, then Jesus enjoyed a special relationship with the God of Israel, the creator of heaven and earth. Indeed, this special relationship with God lay at the heart of Jesus' life and mission. The God of Abraham, the God of Isaac, the God of Jacob was his Father. Jesus was the Son of God. The significance of all that Jesus did and taught arose from his being the Son of God. One of the central themes of John's Gospel is that Jesus' mission was to do his Father's bidding and proclaim his Father's message and so reveal his Father to us:

> Whoever has seen me has seen the Father. How can you say, "Show us the Father"? Do you not believe that I am in the Father and the Father is in me? The words that I say to you I do not speak on my own; but the Father who dwells in me does his works. Believe me that I am in the Father and the Father is in me. (John 14:9–11)

Jesus lived among us as the revelation of the Father. Because he was truly the Son of God, those who saw Jesus saw the Father. Jesus was not merely a messenger of God, as were the Old Testament prophets. Jesus himself was the message of God, the Word of God to us.

Were Jesus not the Son of God, his words and actions would have been presumptuous indeed. Some accused him of blasphemy (see Matthew 26:65) and were angered by the relationship he claimed to have with God: "For this reason the Jews were seeking all the more to kill him, because he was not only breaking the sabbath, but was also calling God his own Father, thereby making himself equal to God" (John 5:18).

But for those who believed in him and accepted his words, Jesus' intimate relationship with God was something they wanted to share in. When the disciples asked Jesus, "Lord, teach us to pray" (Luke 11:1), they were not only asking to be able to pray as he prayed; they were asking to enter into Jesus' intimate relationship with the Father.

For Reflection

- *When do I pray?*
- *What do I usually talk to God about?*

Prayer Starter

Thank you, Lord Jesus Christ, for coming among us as the Son of God. Teach me to pray. Give me the gift and grace of praying as you prayed.

2

God Is Our Father Too

Pray then in this way:
Our Father in heaven,
hallowed be your name.

Matthew 6:9

Were Jesus not the Son of God, his claim of intimacy with the Father would have been blasphemous. No mere man, certainly, could take it upon himself to address God as "Abba"—to approach the creator of the universe with the same familiarity that a son or daughter has with his or her parents.

Yet that is precisely what Jesus invited his disciples to do!

The prayer that Jesus taught his followers, the prayer that we say as the Lord's Prayer, addresses God as "Father," as "our Father." Jesus authorized his disciples to pray as he prayed, to turn to his Father as their Father.

This prayer was not merely a matter of words, a new formula the disciples could use when they prayed. The prayer that Jesus taught his followers reflected a new relationship that he was establishing between them and God. Jesus could authorize his followers to address God as "Father" because his mission was to make them sons and daughters of God.

God as Our Father

Jesus taught us what it means to have God as our Father. The parable of the prodigal son is really the parable of the loving father (see Luke 15:11–32). When we read this parable, we often focus on the son who demanded his inheritance from his father and then squandered it in a foreign land. But the parable has less to do with the son's coming to his senses and returning home than with his father's eagerness to welcome him back. The father forgave his wayward son without quibble or question and celebrated his return with a party. And that, Jesus taught, is what your heavenly Father is like: eager to forgive, eager to welcome us to himself. The parable teaches us about God our Father's love for us and about his joy when we turn to him.

Jesus used the love that human parents have for their children as an example of the way God loves us. He taught that our heavenly Father's love goes far beyond the love that we have for our children. "If you then, who are evil, know how to give good gifts to your children, how much more will your Father in heaven give good things to those who ask him!" (Matthew 7:11). Jesus taught that our heavenly Father knows our every need (see Matthew 6:32) and has prepared an eternal home for us: "Do not be afraid, little flock, for it is your Father's good pleasure to give you the kingdom" (Luke 12:32).

Through his death and resurrection, Jesus made it possible for us to be adopted as children of God. The Son of God came so that we might partake of the relationship with the Father that he himself had: "I am ascending to my Father and your Father, to my God and your God" (John 20:17). Jesus could therefore teach his followers to pray as he prayed because he was inviting them to enter into a relationship with his Father as their Father, calling upon him as their Abba.

The first followers of Jesus spoke Aramaic, so it was natural for them to use the same Aramaic word for *father* that Jesus used when he prayed.

But this practice seems to have persisted in the early church, even among Christians whose native tongue was not Aramaic. When Paul, writing in Greek to Greek-speaking Christians, wished to describe their prayers, he wrote of their calling upon God as Abba:

> For all who are led by the Spirit of God are children of God. For you did not receive a spirit of slavery to fall back into fear, but you have received a spirit of adoption. When we cry, "Abba! Father!" it is that very Spirit bearing witness with our spirit that we are children of God. (Romans 8:14–16)

> And because you are children, God has sent the Spirit of his Son into our hearts, crying, "Abba! Father!" (Galatians 4:6)

Of course, Greek-speaking Christians could (and did) use the Greek word for *father* when they prayed to God as their Father, but at least some of them preserved the memory of the Aramaic word *abba* that Jesus and Aramaic-speaking Christians used in prayer. This practice highlights the significance of praying to God as our Father: we do so in imitation of Jesus, who has enabled us to enter into his relationship with God as his Father.

The Spirit of Adoption

Paul points out that it is through the Holy Spirit that we are able to call God "Abba, Father," for it is through the Spirit that we are adopted as children of God. Jesus also spoke of the Spirit and his role. In John's account of the Last Supper, Jesus told his followers that he was going to leave them, but that did not mean that they would be abandoned: "I will ask the Father, and he will give you another Advocate, to be with you forever. This is the Spirit. . . . I will not leave you orphaned" (John 14:16–18). The apostles would not be left orphans because they would be God's adopted children.

Through the work of Jesus Christ and the presence of the Holy Spirit within us, we are truly adopted as sons and daughters of God. We can therefore address God as "my Father," "Abba"; we can pray as Jesus prayed. What might have been presumptuous for us to do on our own— dare approach the creator of the universe as a child approaches his or her parents—we can do through Jesus Christ. As Paul notes, we do not have to come before God in fear; we are not slaves cringing before a master. We are sons and daughters confidently approaching our Abba, our Father. Through Jesus Christ, we can enter into intimacy with God.

When we pray to God as our Father, we are making a very bold proclamation of who we are: we are claiming to be sons and daughters of God. When we pray, "Our Father," we are speaking from within an intimate relationship with God, a relationship established for us by Jesus Christ. To understand the prayer of Jesus, we must recognize his relationship with God as his Abba. For us to pray as Jesus taught us is to address that same God as our Abba. Jesus, has authorized us to pray as he prayed; he has enabled us to have access to his Father as our Father.

Our prayer is therefore our entering into a relationship with God established for us by Jesus Christ. Our prayer can never be reduced to a technique—to "how-to-do-it instructions" or "rules for success in prayer." Our prayer will always have an element of mystery because prayer is an aspect of our personal relationship with God. Just as we cannot reduce human friendship to set rules or capture the love between a mother and a daughter in an instruction book, so we cannot remove the dimension of mystery from our life of prayer. Just as our relationship with our parents matured as we grew up, and just as our relationship with a spouse or close friend grows over the years, so our relationship with God will change as we grow in our love for him and knowledge of him. This means that our prayer will change also.

For Reflection

- *What words do I most often use to address God?*
- *Do I think of him as my Father?*
- *Am I comfortable calling upon him as my Father?*

Prayer Starter

Abba, dear Father! Teach me how much you love me. Make me comfortable coming into your presence as your dear child.

3

We Are Children of God

Let the little children come to me, and do not stop them; for it is to such as these that the kingdom of God belongs. Truly I tell you, whoever does not receive the kingdom of God as a little child will never enter it.

Luke 18:16–17

What does it mean to receive the kingdom of God like a child? We often focus on the qualities that we presume characterize children, and we think we should imitate those qualities. Children are thought to be innocent, direct in their affections, loving, trusting, spontaneous, joyful, carefree. We in turn try to make these characteristics part of ourselves, usually without complete success.

Parents know that these traits do characterize children, but parents also know that there is another side to the story. Children can also be self-centered, inconsiderate, prey to petty jealousies, indiscriminate in their affections, and inconsistent in their behavior. Most children are not such models of virtue that we can easily understand Jesus' requiring us to imitate them. What, then, did Jesus mean?

To Be Sons and Daughters

The essential characteristic of children that Jesus would have us imitate is their status as sons and daughters. Children may be good children or bad children—but they are still sons and daughters. Nothing changes that basic relationship.

This truth is clearly seen in the parable of the prodigal son in chapter 15 of Luke's Gospel. The prodigal did not act as a good son should have; even after he regretted his sins, he only hoped to return to his father's house as a servant: "I am no longer worthy to be called your son; treat me like one of your hired hands" (verse 19). But the father nevertheless insisted that he was indeed his son and welcomed him home as a son: "Get the fatted calf and kill it, and let us eat and celebrate; for this son of mine was dead and is alive again; he was lost and is found!" (verses 23–24). The prodigal son's sins did not change the basic reality that he was his father's son; nor did they change his father's love for him.

This is the fundamental reality for us as well. Because we have been redeemed by Jesus Christ and given the Holy Spirit, we are adopted as sons and daughters of God and can truly call upon him as our Father (see Romans 8:14–17). It is important for us to acknowledge our adoption as daughters and sons of God. How we behave is also important: parents do not want their children to be ill-mannered or disobedient. But the basic reality is simply that we are God's sons and daughters.

Understood in this light, Jesus' words "Whoever does not receive the kingdom of God as a little child will never enter it" (Luke 18:17) take on a particular meaning. Jesus did not exhort us to adopt childlike character traits or to act childishly. Rather, Jesus asked us to acknowledge the sonship and daughtership that he gives us. The kingdom of heaven is promised to those who call God "Abba, Father," entering into an intimate and loving relationship with God.

Entering into this relationship with God demands some decisions on our part. It requires that we accept God as our Father and turn to him as our Father in love and worship. It requires that we acknowledge his Son, Jesus Christ, as our Savior and Lord and subordinate our own desires to his commands. It requires that we welcome the Holy Spirit into our lives as our guide and our strength.

More is involved in accepting God as our Father and Jesus as our Savior than a simple, once-and-for-all decision. Even after our initial response to God's grace, we may need to deal with attitudes we developed over the years—attitudes that sometimes cripple our prayer life and prevent us from entering into a real relationship with God as our Father. We may have a hard time accepting that we have been truly adopted as sons and daughters of God; we may be hesitant to turn to God in prayer as our Father.

Our Image of God

Often we need to correct our image of God. If we imagine God as an impersonal force that holds the universe in existence, we can hardly consider establishing a personal relationship with him. If we imagine God as someone distant from the world and indifferent to our problems, then we are not going to be able to turn to him in prayer with any real conviction. If we imagine God as a stern judge who carefully notes all our sins and mistakes so that he can bring them against us on judgment day, we will have a hard time approaching him with anything but fear. If these images hold sway in our minds, they block us from freely turning to God in prayer as his children.

Jesus proclaimed a different image of God: God as a loving Father. Jesus told his followers that God is like the father of the prodigal son. Even though the son had in effect said to his father, "I can't wait for you to die; give me my inheritance now," the father never disowned his son, never cut him out of his heart. Even though the son moved far away and wasted his inheritance on sinful pleasure, the father still longed for his return, scanning the horizon from the roof of his house until the day when he saw his son approaching in the distance. At the sight of his son, he "was filled with compassion; he ran and put his arms around him and kissed him" (Luke 15:20). That is the image Jesus gave us of God: the Father filled with compassion, the Father who runs to us, the Father who puts his arms around us and kisses us, even if we have sinned, even if the stench of sin still clings to us, even if we feel completely unworthy to be a daughter or son of this Father.

Yet even if we know that Jesus revealed God to be a loving Father, we can still hesitate to accept him as our Father. Even if we are making a conscious effort to relate to God as our Father, we can still be held back by guilt feelings.

Guilt Feelings

Many of us are very aware of our shortcomings, and we assume that everyone else is also aware of them. We know our mistakes and weaknesses; we know the pain we have caused others, intentionally or unintentionally. While we can cover up our insecurities in front of others, we cannot hide them from God. When we try to enter into his presence, we drag our guilt along with us. We feel uncomfortable in his sight, knowing that he recognizes our every sin and flaw. We feel ashamed, and we vaguely long for someplace to hide.

Yet these feelings run counter to what Jesus taught us about his Father's love for us. A father and mother know their young children are weak; that is why they are in special need of parental love. If children were perfect and self-sufficient in every way, then one aspect of the work of parents would be over. But a mother and father love each child, even in that child's particular needs. Jesus told us that God our Father loves us no less in our particular needs and weaknesses—and indeed loves us a whole lot more than we love our own children: "If you then, who are evil, know how to give good gifts to your children, how much more will your Father in heaven give good things to those who ask him!" (Matthew 7:11).

Jesus accepts our sinfulness as a fact. He deals with us the same way he dealt with the woman caught in adultery. He did not say that she really hadn't sinned. He did say to her, "Neither do I condemn you. Go your way, and from now on do not sin again" (John 8:11).

Despite our sinfulness, Jesus repeatedly proclaimed that his Father loves us. We have a hard time accepting both these truths at the same time: we are sinners, yet God our Father loves us. This is the revelation Jesus came to bring, a revelation he confirmed in his own blood: "God proves his love for us in that while we still were sinners Christ died for us" (Romans 5:8).

The prodigal's father did not hold his son's sins against him but gave even more forgiveness than the son asked for. The father did not allow his son to wallow in his feelings of guilt at having sinned against heaven and his father, but instead he threw a party with great rejoicing. Truly, if we enter into the presence of our heavenly Father with repentance, we do not need to feel guilty.

It is as children, then, that we approach our heavenly Father in prayer. It is as children that we accept his love for us and converse with him as our Father. It is as children that we accept his forgiveness and rejoice that we can be in his presence.

For Reflection

- *Do I draw back from intimacy with God because I know I am unworthy to enter into his presence?*
- *Do I believe that God is nonetheless inviting me to come before him as his beloved child?*

Prayer Starter

Lord Jesus, you want to take me by the hand and lead me to your Father. You want me to acknowledge that I am a child of God and rejoice in my adoption. Thank you for bringing me to your Father.

4

Praying Simply and Directly

*When you are praying, do not heap up empty phrases as
the Gentiles do; for they think that they will be heard
because of their many words. Do not be like them, for
your Father knows what you need before you ask him.*

Pray then in this way:
 Our Father in heaven,
  hallowed be your name.
  Your kingdom come.
  Your will be done,
   on earth as it is in heaven.
  Give us this day our daily bread.
  And forgive us our debts,
   as we also have forgiven our debtors.
  And do not bring us to the time of trial,
   but rescue us from the evil one.

Matthew 6:7–13

Because we are children of God, our conversation with our Father should be marked by certain qualities. These are not so much rules to be followed in prayer as characteristics that flow naturally from our basic relationship with God. Because we are children of God, his cherished sons and daughters, our prayers can be simple and confident, yet marked by determination and obedience. Let us first look at simplicity in prayer.

It is striking that the prayer that Jesus taught his followers is a rather short and simple prayer. Very few of the psalms are shorter than the Lord's Prayer; most of them are considerably longer. The simplicity and directness with which the Lord's Prayer addresses God differ from the rather elaborate way God is addressed in some Jewish prayers. One popular Jewish prayer at the time of Jesus began, "Lord God of Abraham, God of Isaac, God of Jacob; God Most High, Creator of heaven and earth; our Shield and the Shield of our fathers."

In contrast, Jesus taught his followers to simply address God as their Father, and this directness and simplicity carry through in the rest of the prayer. No special preparation is demanded—no preliminary rituals of purification, no incense, no special prayer garments. Jesus taught his disciples to approach God in a direct manner, as a son or daughter approaches a father.

Jesus taught his followers to pray to God as he prayed to his Father, and Jesus prayed with directness and simplicity. The prayers of Jesus in the Gospels have a simplicity to them—even the long prayer that makes up chapter 17 of John's Gospel. We do not find any cumbersome circumlocutions in Jesus' prayers: "I thank you, Father, Lord of heaven and earth, because you have hidden these things from the wise and the intelligent and have revealed them to infants" (Matthew 11:25). "Father, into your hands I commend my spirit" (Luke 23:46). Prayer worthy of God's attention does not have to be lengthy and wordy or a detailed listing of a prescribed number of points.

Jesus' prayers were direct because Jesus was praying to his Father. This is also why we can pray with simplicity: we are praying to our Father. We can use our understanding of human parenthood to gain an insight into God's fatherhood and our prayers as adopted children. How should sons and daughters approach their father or mother? How is their love for each other expressed in their daily conversation?

A Child's Request

We expect children to be respectful toward their parents. A son should honor his father; a daughter should show deference to her mother. It is offensive for a child to treat a parent as an equal, to be flippant with a mother or a father.

At the same time, we do not expect a child to stand in tongue-tied awe in the presence of his or her parents. There should be a free and easy exchange between them; a child should feel comfortable and loved in the presence of his or her father and mother. A child should be able to express gratitude for the good things that a parent provides, but this is normally done more by hugs and smiles than by formal thank-you notes. A child should be able to ask for the things he or she needs, but ask simply. It would be bewildering if a son said to his father, "Oh, father of mine, beneficent and kindly, deign to hear my humble petition for a new baseball, for verily, my old one has come apart at the seams." We expect, rather, that he would say, "Dad, could I please have a new baseball? My old one is falling apart."

Jesus would have us approach his Father in the same respectful, simple, direct way. There is no need for us to multiply words endlessly; God knows our needs. There is no need to couch our prayers in artificial formal language; our heavenly Father knows our hearts. When we turn to God in prayer, we can pray a rather simple prayer: "Our Father in heaven, hallowed be your name. . . ."

All our prayers can share the directness of the Lord's Prayer. We can express our sorrow to God when we are sorrowful, our joy when we are joyful, our contrition when we are contrite. Our prayers should express the true thoughts of our minds and feelings of our hearts. We should not hide behind an elaborate construction of words in the mistaken belief that they are more pleasing to God. We should pray with words that are natural to us and really express what we think and how we feel. Our prayers are no less worshipful for being simple and honest.

Jesus, One of Us

Jesus allowed and encouraged such a simple and direct approach to him. The Son of God did not come among us with the splendor and pomp of a king, although such honors would have been due him. His glory was revealed once, during his transfiguration on the mountain, but afterward he instructed his apostles to say nothing about it until after his resurrection (see Matthew 17:9). The normal appearance of Jesus was as a common man, and those who knew him spoke to him as they would to another man.

Those without faith in Jesus, including those from his hometown, were baffled that such an ordinary-looking person could do what Jesus did: "Where did this man get this wisdom and these deeds of power? Is not this the carpenter's son?" (Matthew 13:54–55). Some of his relatives could not accept him as being other than an ordinary person, and "they went out to restrain him, for people were saying, 'He has gone out of his mind'" (Mark 3:21). Those who saw him through the eyes of faith approached him with respect as well as friendship but still spoke with him in a simple and direct way. Peter even reacted to Jesus' prediction of his coming death by trying to talk him out of it (see Matthew 16:22).

Even after his resurrection, the glorified body of Jesus was apparently not all light and splendor. Mary Magdalene, who certainly knew Jesus well, mistook him for a gardener (see John 20:15). Jesus walked with two of his disciples for several miles on the road to Emmaus, and they simply thought he was a stranger until they recognized him in the breaking of the bread (see Luke 24:35). Jesus revealed himself to the apostles by cooking a fish breakfast for them (see John 21:9–13). How ordinary!

The Right Words

Just as Jesus allowed his friends easy access to him, so he taught them to approach his Father in a simple and direct way. He tried to instill confidence in them, confidence that when they turned to their Father in prayer, he would hear them.

Jesus told his followers that they would be dragged before kings and courts of law for his sake, a prospect that might normally terrify simple, uneducated people. But Jesus also told them not to worry when it happened: "When they hand you over, do not worry about how you are to speak or what you are to say; for what you are to say will be given to you at that time; for it is not you who speak, but the Spirit of your Father speaking through you" (Matthew 10:19–20).

If followers of Jesus can speak confidently before kings, how much more confidently can we speak to our Father! If the Holy Spirit inspires us to bear witness to those who are hostile, how much more will he inspire us to pray to the God who loves us! If we can speak with assurance before courts of law, how much more confidently can we approach our Father in his heavenly courts!

Paul writes, "Likewise the Spirit helps us in our weakness; for we do not know how to pray as we ought, but that very Spirit intercedes with sighs too deep for words. And God, who searches the heart, knows what is the mind of the Spirit, because the Spirit intercedes for the saints according to the will of God" (Romans 8:26–27).

We can rely on the inspiration of the Holy Spirit when we go before our Father in prayer. We can offer our simple prayers with confidence, knowing that we are praying to a Father who loves us. We can approach God directly and with trust, for that is how Jesus prayed, and that is how he taught us to pray.

For Reflection

- *Do I speak with God simply and directly, as a child to a parent?*
- *What is holding me back from greater intimacy with God and from greater freedom in his presence?*

Prayer Starter

Father, give me the grace of coming before you as your child, joyful in your presence. Send your Holy Spirit upon me to unite me with you and your Son, Jesus, and to give me words of prayer.

5

Praying with Confidence

Jesus looked upward and said, "Father, I thank you for having heard me. I knew that you always hear me, but I have said this for the sake of the crowd standing here, so that they may believe that you sent me." When he had said this, he cried with a loud voice, "Lazarus, come out!"

John 11:41–43

Jesus prayed with confidence. When he turned to his Father in prayer, he knew that what he asked would be granted. Even if he prayed for a great miracle—the raising of a dead man back to life—he knew his Father would hear him.

Even at the time of his arrest in the Garden of Gethsemane, Jesus knew that the Father was by his side and would honor his prayer. There was no need for Peter to draw his sword in a futile attempt to protect Jesus from the soldiers. Jesus said that if he wanted to he could "appeal to my Father, and he will at once send me more than twelve legions of angels" (Matthew 26:53).

Jesus instructed his followers to pray with a similar confidence, to turn to God with a firm and sure faith:

> Have faith in God. Truly I tell you, if you say to this mountain, "Be taken up and thrown into the sea," and if you do not doubt in your heart, but believe that what you say will come to pass, it will be done for you. So I tell you, whatever you ask for in prayer, believe that you have received it, and it will be yours. (Mark 11:22–24)

These words are disturbing, for Jesus seems to have promised too much. Jesus did not draw a distinction between things we should pray for and things we should not pray for; he did not hedge his promise by saying that our prayers will be answered most of the time. Rather, Jesus told his followers, "All things can be done for the one who believes" (Mark 9:23). He told them, "I will do whatever you ask in my name" (John 14:13). He promised them, "If you abide in me, and my words abide in you, ask for whatever you wish, and it will be done for you. . . . The Father will give you whatever you ask him in my name" (John 15:7, 16). How are we to understand such sweeping promises?

Praying with Faith

Jesus did place one condition on these promises: we must pray with faith. "Whatever you ask for in prayer with faith, you will receive" (Matthew 21:22). Even a rather modest amount of faith can do wonders: "If you had faith the size of a mustard seed, you could say to this mulberry tree, 'Be uprooted and planted in the sea,' and it would obey you" (Luke 17:6). A lack of faith blocks effective prayer; the presence of faith makes all things possible. When the disciples asked Jesus why they were unable to cast out a demon, Jesus answered, "Because of your little faith. For truly I tell you, if you have faith the size of a mustard seed, you will say to this mountain, 'Move from here to there,' and it will move; and nothing will be impossible for you" (Matthew 17:20).

The letter of James echoes the need for faith. When we turn to God with a request, we must "ask in faith, never doubting, for the one who doubts is like a wave of the sea, driven and tossed by the wind; for the doubter, being double-minded and unstable in every way, must not expect to receive anything from the Lord" (1:6–8).

These are two-edged promises. At the same time, they call us to grow in faith, and they reveal how little faith we have. They command us to get over our doubts but make it all too obvious just how many doubts we harbor and how ineffective our faith is in overcoming them.

It is a mistake, however, to focus on our faith as if it were merely a quality of ours, a measure of our inner strength and resolve. It is a mistake to focus on our doubts and try to banish them by sheer willpower. We need, rather, to focus on the basis of our faith: the revelation of God brought to us in Jesus Christ. We need to overcome our doubts, not by dwelling on them, but by paying attention to what Jesus told us about his Father.

Faith in the Father's Love

Jesus revealed that God is our Father. The basis of our praying with faith is not some magical strength within us; rather, because God is our Father, we can turn to him with confidence. Jesus prayed to his Father with complete confidence; he taught us to pray the same way.

When we pray to God, we are praying to a Father who already knows our needs and loves us:

> Therefore I tell you, do not worry about your life, what you will eat or what you will drink, or about your body, what you will wear. Is not life more than food, and the body more than clothing? Look at the birds of the air; they neither sow nor reap nor gather into barns, and yet your heavenly Father feeds them. Are you not of more value than they? . . . Therefore do not worry, saying, "What will we eat?" or "What will we to drink?" or "What will we wear?" For it is the Gentiles who strive for all these things; and indeed your heavenly Father knows that you need all these things. (Matthew 6:25–26, 31–32)

Our Father cares for the birds of the air and the flowers of the field; not a single sparrow falls to the ground without the Father knowing it (see Matthew 10:29). We are his children, and he cares for us more than all the sparrows in the world. It is because God loves us as a Father and is concerned about our needs that we can pray to him with trust and simplicity. "Your Father knows what you need before you ask him" (Matthew 6:8).

God's love for us extends far beyond merely meeting our minimum needs for physical survival. "Do not be afraid, little flock, for it is your Father's good pleasure to give you the kingdom" (Luke 12:32). There is something almost humorous about this promise. The band of fishermen, housewives, and minor civil servants who straggled after Jesus does not strike us as the stuff of which kingdoms are made. Yet Jesus promised this ragtag collection of people the kingdom of God. Clearly, God's gifts are not limited by the status or merits of those to whom he gives them.

The Father's Gift

Jesus revealed that God is a loving Father; this is the basis of our confidence in prayer. We can pray with faith because we are praying to our heavenly Father. Faith, in fact, is one of our Father's gifts to us!

> Ask, and it will be given you; search, and you will find; knock, and the door will be opened for you. For everyone who asks receives, and everyone who searches finds, and for everyone who knocks, the door will be opened. Is there anyone among you who, if your child asks for bread, will

give a stone? Or if the child asks for a fish, will give a snake? If you then, who are evil, know how to give good gifts to your children, how much more will your Father in heaven give good things to those who ask him! (Matthew 7:7–11)

When we pray in faith, we pray as children, not as spiritual supermen or superwomen. We turn to God with confidence, not because of any qualities within us, but because God is a Father who gives good gifts. Our confidence is not in ourselves or in our faith or in our prayer; our confidence lies in our Father's unbounded love for us. We know how we love our children, despite our failings and sins; Jesus taught us that God's love for his children is immeasurably greater.

How do we respond to our children's requests? We obviously do not give them everything they ask for. If an eight-year-old boy wants a thirty-foot racing boat for Christmas, even a wealthy father will temper his request, knowing that no matter how attractive a boat may be to his son, it would not be a safe present for him. But on the other hand, a parent will do everything imaginable to meet a child's real need. If a child is struck by a car, a mother will immediately rush to the emergency room to be by the child's bedside. If the injury requires expensive medical treatment, no sacrifice is too great; the father will willingly remortgage the house or take a second job in order to get the money.

God's love for us is a parent's love. We may not always understand why God chooses to give us some things and withhold others, but we can be confident that God's choices are made out of his fatherly love for us, just as we take loving care of our children.

A parent provides not only the essentials but also the extras—gifts that will bring a child joy. Most important, a parent provides love; even expensive gifts are empty without love. God's love for us is a father's love—and it is beyond a human father's love because God is *the* Father. It is from this perspective that we can understand Jesus' promises that our prayers will be answered. Because God loves us as our Father, "this is the boldness we have in him, that if we ask anything according to his will, he hears us" (1 John 5:14). Therefore, we can pray to him with confidence and peace. Therefore, Paul could write to the Philippians, "Do not worry about anything, but in everything by prayer and supplication with thanksgiving let your requests be made known to God. And the peace of God, which surpasses all understanding, will guard your hearts and your minds in Christ Jesus" (Philippians 4:6–7).

For Reflection

- *How have I experienced God's fatherly care?*
- *Do I believe that he cares about me even more than the most loving of human parents care for their child?*

Prayer Starter

Thank you, my Father in heaven, for loving me far more than I deserve or can even imagine. Teach me to rely on your love and to entrust myself into your arms as my Father.

6

Finding a Time and a Place to Pray

In the morning, while it was still very dark, [Jesus] got up and went out to a deserted place, and there he prayed. And Simon and his companions hunted for him. When they found him, they said to him, "Everyone is searching for you."

Mark 1:35–37

The Gospels tell us that Jesus regularly spent time with his Father in prayer. That a son talked often with his father should not surprise us. However, what is striking about the Gospel accounts of Jesus' prayer is the difficulty Jesus had in finding the time and place to pray and his determination in overcoming these obstacles.

We find Jesus in prayer at all the key points in his life. In Luke's account of Jesus' baptism by John, "Jesus also had been baptized and was praying, the heaven was opened, and the Holy

Spirit descended upon him in bodily form like a dove. And a voice came from heaven, 'You are my Son, the Beloved; with you I am well pleased'" (Luke 3:21–22). This event marked the beginning of Jesus' public ministry, yet he did not immediately set out to preach his good news or call followers. He first went into the desert for forty days of prayer and fasting.

It was in prayer that he chose the twelve apostles: "During those days he went out to the mountain to pray; and he spent the night in prayer to God. And when day came, he called his disciples and chose twelve of them, whom he also named apostles" (Luke 6:12–13). It was while Jesus was praying on a mountain that he was transfigured: "While he was praying, the appearance of his face changed, and his clothes became dazzling white" (Luke 9:29). It was in prayer that he contemplated and accepted death for our sakes (see Matthew 26:36–46).

Yet despite the importance Jesus placed on prayer, a life of prayer did not come easily for him. He had to overcome many obstacles to prayer—obstacles that arose from the lifestyle that his mission demanded.

The Press of the Crowds

Jesus attracted crowds wherever he went. One time the crowds were so dense that a crippled man on a stretcher could not be brought into the house where Jesus was teaching but had to be lowered into Jesus' presence through a hole punched in the roof (see Luke 5:17–26). Sometimes the crowds were so numerous that simply feeding them became a problem (see Luke 9:12–17). Crowds were almost constantly in the background during the public ministry of Jesus, crowds seeking his teaching, crowds coming to him with their needs. "Then he went home; and the crowd came together again, so that they could not even eat" (Mark 3:19–20).

When Jesus and the apostles wished to be alone, they had to sneak away—a tactic that did not always work:

He said to them, "Come away to a deserted place all by yourselves and rest a while." For many were coming and going, and they had no leisure even to eat. And they went away in the boat to a deserted place by themselves. Now many saw them going and recognized them, and they hurried there on foot from all the towns and arrived ahead of them.

> As he went ashore, he saw a great crowd; and he had compassion for them, because they were like sheep without a shepherd; and he began to teach them many things. (Mark 6:31–34)

Such a lifestyle was hardly conducive to prayer. Our image of a life oriented to prayer is a life of unhurried pace, regular schedule, silence, solitude. In contrast, the life of Jesus resembled that of a presidential candidate in the midst of a campaign: always in the public eye, never far from the clamor of the crowds, continually traveling from one place to another: "The Son of Man has nowhere to lay his head" (Luke 9:58).

Yet Jesus did spend time in prayer. "Many crowds would gather to hear him and to be cured of their diseases. But he would withdraw to deserted places and pray" (Luke 5:15–16). Sometimes he would send the apostles and the crowd on ahead while he would go up into the hills to pray (see Mark 6:45–46). Sometimes he stayed up late, praying far into the night—or even through the night (see Luke 6:12). Sometimes he arose very early: "In the morning, while it was still very dark, he got up and went out to a deserted place, and there he prayed" (Mark 1:35).

Jesus had the same trouble finding time to pray that we have. He was not a first-century superman—able to go without food or sleep in a way that we ourselves cannot. Our reverence for the divinity of Jesus Christ should not blind us to his full humanity. He experienced hunger as we experience hunger; he felt the stones of the road through his sandals. When Jesus and his disciples walked from Judea to Galilee—a distance of about seventy miles—he became "tired out by his journey" (John 4:6). He asked the Samaritan woman at the well for a drink of water because he was truly thirsty, just as we would be thirsty after a long hike on a hot day. If Jesus could sleep through a storm at sea (see Luke 8:23), he could indeed know the fatigue that sometimes makes us fall into our beds exhausted.

Therefore, when Jesus spent the whole night in prayer, he had to sacrifice sleep and battle fatigue, just as we would have to do. When Jesus rose early in the morning to pray, it took resolve on his part, a determination to make time for communion with his Father. Jesus was without sin and enjoyed intimate union with the Father—yet he was fully and truly human. "The Word became flesh" (John 1:14), our flesh, subject to fatigue, "in every respect . . . tested as we are" (Hebrews 4:15).

Finding a Time and a Place

We can learn the way of prayer from Jesus and draw encouragement from his life of prayer. If we must contend with erratic schedules and the demands of family life, Jesus had to contend with even greater demands. If the pace of modern life seems too rapid to allow us the luxury of prayer, the public ministry of Jesus was no less hectic. If we have trouble finding a quiet place to be alone with God, Jesus experienced the same difficulty. If our work demands much of us, Jesus' ministry demanded no less of him.

For many of us, one of the biggest obstacles to prayer is simply finding the time. Perhaps we should admit that there is no perfect time in our day for prayer and then select a definite time anyway. It may mean getting up twenty minutes earlier in the morning and dedicating the quiet time before breakfast to prayer. It may mean using the lull after the last child has left for school for time alone with God. It may mean finding a place of solitude during lunch hour. The ideal would be for us to have a regular time for prayer in our daily schedules.

Finding a time and sticking to it may be difficult, but it is clear that Jesus would have us commit ourselves to prayer with firm determination. His parables about persistence in prayer are not parables about God's slowness to hear our prayers; they are parables about our need for steadfastness. Jesus told a story about a man who had unexpected company and needed to borrow three loaves of bread from a sleeping neighbor. This parable occurs in the context of Jesus' teaching his followers to pray the Our Father to a God who has a Father's eagerness to answer their prayers (see Luke 11:1–13). The point of this parable is that we must be persistent in prayer, just as the man was persistent in pounding on the door and asking for bread. The parable of the widow who beseeched the unscrupulous judge (see Luke 18:1–8) teaches us the "need to pray always and not to lose heart" (Luke 18:1). Jesus contrasted God's generous justice with this judge's grudging action but still exhorted persistence and determination in prayer.

Making a Commitment

We do not have to wear down God's reluctance to hear us by unending begging; Jesus asserted that it is those who do not know God as their Father who take such an approach (see Matthew 6:7–8). Jesus taught that our Father knows our needs even before we ask, and we therefore do not need to multiply words. Nonetheless, we need to have a firm commitment to pray; we need to be steadfast in our prayer; we need to be determined to pray despite whatever obstacles we may encounter.

The example of Jesus should also reassure us. We should not feel guilty because our prayer time is irregular—because our day is fragmented by hundreds of demands, because our schedule is ruined by traffic jams, because distractions make constant assaults on our minds. Jesus knows that our life is not the life of a hermit. He will understand our failures if we do our best to make time for prayer with the same determination he showed in finding time to be with his Father.

For Reflection

- *How faithful am I to daily prayer?*
- *When is the best time during my day for me to set aside some moments to be alone with God?*

Prayer Starter

Father, you know my good intentions—and how I fall short of carrying them out. Give me the grace to stick with my resolve to spend time every day with you in prayer.

7

Prayer That Makes a Difference

Not everyone who says to me, "Lord, Lord," will enter the kingdom of heaven, but only the one who does the will of my Father in heaven.

Matthew 7:21

The complexity of our lives often leads to the compartmentalization of our lives. We switch from role to role in the course of a day, almost from identity to identity. How many long-suffering employees at work become grouchy spouses at home?

We can fall into the habit of making prayer one of the compartments of our lives. We spend our quiet moments communing with God, communing even with fervor. But once our time of prayer is over, we go back to our ordinary lives, falling prey to our habitual temptations, putting ourselves and our interests first.

Jesus warned us that no amount of crying out to him as Lord will substitute for carrying out God's will in our lives. Prayer should dispose us to obedience, not dispense us from it. We know this but still find ourselves falling short. What are we to do?

As in every aspect of prayer, we can look to the example of Jesus and try to learn from it. Here too Jesus has much to teach us. Jesus' relationship with his Father was not merely a matter of acknowledging him in prayer several times a day. Jesus was the Son of God in all that he did and all that he said, all the hours of the day.

John's Gospel highlights Jesus' relationship with God as his Father. One of John's themes is that Jesus was sent by God to the world. Jesus did not claim to be acting on his own initiative or authority, but he maintained that he had been sent by God with a mission to carry out: "I have not come on my own" (John 7:28). Jesus claimed to have an intimate bond with his Father (see John 16:32). He proclaimed himself to be God's Son (see John 10:36). He even boldly claimed, "The Father and I are one" (John 10:30). He based his authority on his relationship with his Father; he justified his mission as being the mission given to him by God.

Therefore, the message that Jesus proclaimed to the world was not his own message but a message given to him by his Father: "My teaching is not mine but his who sent me" (John 7:16). "I have not spoken on my own, but the Father who sent me has himself given me a commandment about what to say and what to speak. . . . What I speak, therefore, I speak just as the Father has told me" (John 12:49–50).

Likewise, Jesus' deeds were deeds done on behalf of the Father. They were "the works that the Father has given me to complete" (John 5:36). Jesus did not claim credit for the signs he performed; they were the works of his Father. He had zeal to be about his Father's business, even if it meant missing a meal: "My food is to do the will of him who sent me and to complete his work" (John 4:34). Jesus felt an urgency to accomplish his Father's mission (see John 9:4).

Jesus acknowledged that he could do nothing on his own: "Very truly, I tell you, the Son can do nothing on his own, but only what he sees the Father doing; for whatever the Father does, the Son does likewise. The Father loves the Son and shows him all that he himself is doing" (John 5:19–20; see also John 8:28–29).

The Father's Will

Jesus did the will of the Father in all things: "I have come down from heaven, not to do my own will, but the will of him who sent me" (John 6:38). Even though he and the Father were united by the strongest bonds of love, Jesus viewed himself as a servant to his Father, subject to the Father's will. Jesus even considered himself bound by the commandments of God (see John 15:10).

Jesus' prayers expressed this basic relationship with the Father. Through prayer, Jesus learned the Father's will for him and committed himself to carrying out that will. Through prayer, Jesus pondered the message of the Father that he was to proclaim to the world. Through prayer, Jesus discerned the works of the Father that he was to perform.

If Jesus' prayers had not borne fruit in his life, then Jesus would not have been the perfect Son of the Father that he was. His relationship with his Father had to be lived out in the works he performed and the message he proclaimed; the love of his heart had to be expressed in deeds and action. No matter how rewarding Jesus' times of prayer might have been, they were only one aspect of his perfect sonship to his Father.

Imitating Jesus' Sonship

The same is true for us. We acknowledge that God is our Father not merely in our prayers but also through our entire lives. We are called to a relationship with God that embraces our whole life; our prayers are merely one aspect of this relationship.

While Jesus proclaimed a message of the Father's love, he also taught the necessity of obedience to the Father's will. His message to his followers during his last meal with them before his death contained a recurring insistence on obedience: "They who have my commandments and keep them are those who love me; and those who love me will be loved by my Father" (John 14:21). In this, Jesus was merely asking us to imitate him in his obedience to his Father: "If you keep my commandments, you will abide in my love, just as I have kept my Father's commandments and abide in his love" (John 15:10).

Thus the relationship with God as our Father that Jesus invited us into includes our obedience to the Father's will. We cannot join with Jesus in his sonship to the Father unless we try to imitate him in his obedience to the Father. The Father's family is made up of those who do his will: "Whoever does the will of my Father in heaven is my brother and sister and mother" (Matthew 12:50).

Therefore, simply crying out to God in prayer is not enough: "Not everyone who says to me, 'Lord, Lord,' will enter the kingdom of heaven, but only the one who does the will of my Father in heaven" (Matthew 7:21). Our prayers cannot be divorced from our life; we must imitate Jesus' eagerness to obey as well as his eagerness to pray. Jesus used a parable to convey the importance of following through on what we say to God:

> "What do you think? A man had two sons; he went to the first and said, 'Son, go and work in the vineyard today.' He answered, 'I will not'; but later he changed his mind and went. The father went to the second and said the same; and he answered, 'I go, sir'; but he did not go. Which of the two did the will of his father?" They said, "The first." (Matthew 21:28–31)

True sons and daughters of God are not those who claim that they intend to do their Father's will but then fail to do it. Rather, true sons and daughters actually carry out their Father's will—perhaps after having wrestled with it in prayer and resisted accepting what they know is God's will for them.

Our prayer is merely one aspect of our imitating Christ and following the path he has established to the Father. The relationship with God we nurture in prayer must bear fruit in the rest of our lives. The thoughts of our hearts in prayer must be expressed by obedience to God's will. Our deeds must become the deeds of children of God, just as our words become the words of sons and daughters. We cannot pray as Jesus prayed unless we obey as Jesus obeyed.

For Reflection

- *How well do I actually carry out the good intentions I have in prayer?*
- *How committed am I to obeying God in all that he asks of me?*

Prayer Starter

Lord Jesus Christ, you are the perfect Son of your Father. Strengthen me so that I might imitate you and be the child of God that your Father invites me to be.

8

---•---

Seeking Forgiveness

And forgive us our sins,
for we ourselves forgive everyone indebted to us.

Luke 11:4

Jesus taught that his Father is compassionate and forgiving, eager to accept a sinner's repentance. Indeed, the Father sent the Son to earth precisely to bring forgiveness: "God did not send the Son into the world to condemn the world, but in order that the world might be saved through him" (John 3:17). God also commands us to forgive others as he forgives us. This command has particular bearing on our prayer.

Jesus taught us to pray, "Forgive us our sins, for we ourselves forgive everyone indebted to us" (Luke 11:4).

Asking for forgiveness in prayer is linked to forgiving those who are in need of forgiveness from us. After teaching his followers the prayer that we call the Our Father, Jesus added the admonition "If you forgive others their trespasses, your heavenly Father will also forgive you; but if you do not forgive others, neither will your Father forgive your trespasses" (Matthew 6:14–15). We cannot pray for forgiveness unless we are willing to grant forgiveness.

Jesus emphasized the necessity of forgiving others. It is the point of the parable about the servant who was forgiven a huge debt by his master but refused to forgive a small debt that was owed to him (see Matthew 18:23–35). The master learned of his servant's hard-heartedness and had him thrown into prison until he repaid his original debt. The parable ends with a somber warning for all who refuse to forgive as they have been forgiven: "So my heavenly Father will also do to every one of you, if you do not forgive your brother or sister from your heart" (Matthew 18:35). Jesus insisted our forgiveness must be given without limit: "not seven times, but, I tell you, seventy-seven times" (Matthew 18:22).

Our willingness to forgive is so important for our prayer that Jesus taught that even if someone was in the middle of presenting an offering at the temple and suddenly remembered a conflict with a brother, he should leave his offering where it was and go to become reconciled with his brother before proceeding further (see Matthew 5:23–24). When Jesus taught about faith and confidence in prayer, his teaching ended with the instruction "Whenever you stand praying, forgive, if you have anything against anyone; so that your Father in heaven may also forgive you your trespasses" (Mark 11:25).

Why did Jesus place such importance on forgiving others? Why did he connect our willingness to forgive with our ability to pray properly?

Praying to a Forgiving God

Forgiveness is important precisely because our prayer is not a mere matter of words and formalities. Our prayer is turning to our heavenly Father in order to grow in union with him. Because God is a forgiving God, we must become forgiving people if we are to be his children.

The revelation that Jesus brought us is that God is our Father and loves us with a Father's love. He did not reveal God to be a prosecutor who scrutinizes our lives to find enough evidence to condemn us. There will be a judgment one day, but our Father is primarily interested in finding repentance in us, not guilt. Hence he provides many opportunities for repentance, and he accepts even the feeble efforts of our hearts to love him.

Once again, it is important to ponder the message of the parable of the prodigal son (see Luke 15:11–32). The father in the parable had been clearly wronged and insulted by his son, yet the father still loved his son and awaited his return. The son only hoped to be accepted back as a servant, but the father insisted on giving him full welcome as a son, clothing him in a fine robe and throwing a party to celebrate his return. It was as if the father were welcoming home a son who had won some kind of national acclaim and high honors—not a son who had wasted his father's money on dissolute living.

Jesus' message was that God is like that father. The image of God that is to be foremost in our minds is the image of a loving father who always stands ready to forgive, no matter what we have done. Nor is the Father's forgiveness grudgingly given; it is full forgiveness, full welcome home. When we do come to our senses and return home, our Father wants to throw a party on our behalf—like the father of the prodigal son, like the shepherd who found his lost sheep, like the woman who found the money that she had lost. All three of these parables are parables of God's mercy, and all three end with the sounds of rejoicing (see Luke 15:6–7, 9–10, 23–25, 32).

God's love is not reserved for only those who deserve it:

> But I say to you, Love your enemies and pray for those who persecute you, so that you may be children of your Father in heaven; for he makes his sun rise on the evil and on the good, and sends rain on the righteous and on the unrighteous. . . . Be perfect, therefore, as your heavenly Father is perfect. (Matthew 5:44–45, 48)

God seems guilty of indiscriminate love. He does not seem to distinguish between those who deserve to have the sun shine upon them and those who do not, between those who deserve rain for their crops and those who deserve drought. Jesus even indicated that God's very perfection lies in loving those who are unlovable. Anyone can love those who return love, but godlike love is for those who do not deserve love (see Matthew 5:46–48).

Forgiveness for All

Jesus wants us to imitate his Father. As God's sons and daughters, we too are called to an indiscriminate love—not merely loving those who deserve our love or return our love, but loving the undeserving as our heavenly Father does. Such love readily grants forgiveness. If we do not insist that others earn our love, then their failures cannot diminish our love for them. If our aim is to love as God loves, then it is natural to forgive as God forgives: "Be merciful, just as your Father is merciful. . . . Forgive, and you will be forgiven" (Luke 6:36–37).

Such forgiveness may require some attitude changes on our part. We must be willing to let go of our grudges; we must be willing to burn the mental scorecards where we have noted the mistakes of others. If we forgive someone for something, then we can no longer dwell on what he or she did or act on the basis of it.

We must also convey our forgiveness to the other person. We must take the first step toward reconciliation, not waiting for the offending party to approach us or admit fault first (see Matthew 5:23–24). We must express our forgiveness to them so that they are not left guessing where they stand with us. We must mean our words of forgiveness, and then we must relate to the other person in the future on the basis of the forgiveness that we have given. We must do this even if all our own feelings are not yet under control. We can control the way we behave more easily than we can control the way we feel, and it is our behavior that is more important.

Forgiveness Means Freedom

Granting forgiveness is a freeing experience. It frees the other person to relate to us in friendship again; it frees us from the frustration and hostility we may have been carrying around inside us. This freedom affects our prayers. We cannot approach God our Father with full freedom and ease if we are harboring grudges in the corner of our souls. We cannot enter fully into the presence of God if we know we are dragging along things that we do not want our Father to see.

One of Jesus' last prayers to his Father was a prayer of forgiveness. He uttered it from the cross, and he uttered it on behalf of those who were putting him to death in the most cruel and humiliating way they knew. Jesus prayed for them in the manner of a defense lawyer at a trial:

he pleaded ignorance on their behalf. Jesus prayed as a son asking a special favor from his father, knowing that the mercy he was asking for was not something these men deserved, but asking nonetheless. Jesus offered a prayer that expressed his own forgiveness of these men: "Father, forgive them; for they do not know what they are doing" (Luke 23:34).

Jesus invited us to pray as he prayed and to forgive as he forgave. He invited us not only to forgive others but also to pray for their forgiveness by God. The ultimate test of whether we have forgiven someone is whether we are willing to sincerely pray that they receive mercy and forgiveness and blessings from God. To pray such a prayer of forgiveness is to pray as Jesus prayed.

For Reflection

- *Am I holding any grudges?*
- *Is there anyone I need to forgive?*
- *Is there anyone whose forgiveness I need to seek?*

Prayer Starter

Thank you, Lord Jesus, for giving your life so that I may be forgiven. Give me the grace to forgive as I have been forgiven.

9

Praying for What We Need Today

Give us this day our daily bread.

Matthew 6:11

M ost of us enjoy some measure of financial security, at least to the extent of not having to worry where our next meal is coming from. A loaf of bread ranks low on our list of needs and seems hardly something to bring to God's attention. There are weightier matters to bring before God in prayer: a relative who is seriously ill, a friend whose marriage is disintegrating, peace in the world. We can pray wholeheartedly for the coming of God's kingdom; we find it a little awkward to pray each day for our lunch. When there are so many important matters demanding God's attention, it seems foolish to bother him about our own trivial needs. To pray for the truly hungry throughout the world would make more sense.

Yet Jesus instructed his followers to make this simple request and to make it daily: "Give us this day our daily bread." As with every aspect of prayer, the key to understanding a request for our daily bread lies in understanding it in light of our relationship with God as our Father.

A Child's Dependence

A young child depends totally on his or her parents for food, clothing, shelter, love, and all other needs. Children recognize this, automatically turning to their parents for their every need. If a dress is torn, Mommy will mend it. When a toy is broken, Daddy will fix it. If there is a thunderstorm, children run to their parents for protection. If children are hungry, they ask their parents for food.

As we grow up, we become progressively free from this total dependency on our parents. We learn to care for ourselves and provide for our needs. We also learn that there are some elements of brokenness in our lives that not even Mommy can mend or Daddy can fix.

Quite early we learn that bread comes from supermarkets or bakeries. We still pray, "Give us this day our daily bread," but we know that when we need bread, we make a trip to the grocery store to buy more. Our prayer may begin to lose some of its meaning, without our realizing it.

Our sense of dependency on our heavenly Father may also fade, just as our dependency on our human parents fades away. Our recourse to God may become less frequent. In times of extreme need, we might remember to pray, but for simpler matters, we largely ignore God and rely on our own resources.

We may even fall into thinking that our prayers make little real difference. If our lives are going well, it is because we are naturally decent people, trying to be good. If we have the material things we need, it is because we hold a steady job and work hard. Prayer might be a good thing, but we are tempted to believe that it really doesn't make all that much difference.

Jesus taught us otherwise. Jesus taught us that behind the obvious laws of cause and effect, there is a God who cares—his Father. He introduced us to his Father as our Father, a God whose loving providence embraces all the laws of the universe without being bound by them. The Father of Jesus is a Father who lovingly cares for us, who even knows how many hairs we have on our heads. He is a Father who wants us to turn to him when we have a cold as well as when we have cancer and who is concerned about every aspect of our lives, minor as well as major. He is a Father who welcomes our continually turning to him, day after day, for even the most trivial matters, even for our daily bread.

God's Love Is Total

Why do we need to petition God for such small favors as daily bread? Behind such seemingly trivial prayers lies a basic truth: God's love for us is total, and we are totally dependent on him. Jesus was also dependent on his Father. If anyone ever lived who had the power to be self-sufficient, it was Jesus Christ—yet he confessed, "I can do nothing on my own" (John 5:30). He acknowledged that he drew his life from his Father (see John 6:57). He showed this dependence on his Father even in the simplest elements of his life—even in his giving thanks to the Father for bread and fish before he ate them or shared them with others (see John 6:11).

When Jesus taught us to pray, "Give us this day our daily bread," he was teaching us to pray as he himself prayed to his Father. He was teaching us to acknowledge our total dependence on God, a dependence we can never outgrow any more than Jesus outgrew his dependence on his Father. He was teaching us that his Father's love extends to even the most seemingly trivial elements of our lives. He was teaching us to turn to his Father for even our simplest needs, as he turned to his Father in all things. He was teaching us how to behave as children of God.

Daily Bread

Our asking for daily bread can have additional meaning. The word *bread* in Scripture can carry the broader meaning of food in general. And in turn, Jesus gave a fuller meaning to *food:*

> Meanwhile the disciples were urging him, "Rabbi, eat something." But he said to them, "I have food to eat that you do not know about." So the disciples said to one another, "Surely no one has brought him something to eat?" Jesus said to them, "My food is to do the will of him who sent me and to complete his work." (John 4:31–34)

What sustained Jesus was not so much the food he consumed each day but the carrying out of his Father's will. So too for us: we can make our prayer for daily bread a prayer asking for the food of doing God's will that day, for the gift of being able to serve God, for the blessing of seeing value in our day's work.

This is not something to take for granted. Many people have trouble seeing that what they do each day makes much difference for the coming of God's kingdom on earth. Much of what we do is simply what we need to do. To pray for our daily bread can then be a prayer that we will understand the meaning of what we must do, however humble it might be, in light of God's plan of salvation for the world. That would be true sustenance for us; that would keep us going through the day.

Praying for the daily sustaining bread of doing God's will can also be a prayer that we will be God's servants in whatever circumstances we find ourselves. It can be a prayer that God will give us openings to serve him that day, and open our eyes to the opportunities that he sends. It can be a prayer that we will imitate Jesus, whose food was to carry out the work of his Father and our Father. "Give us this day our daily bread" can encompass all that we need this day to satisfy our hunger and sustain us on our journey to our Father.

For Reflection

- *How do I acknowledge my dependence on God?*
- *How do I express my trust in his loving concern for me?*
- *What is the bread I need today?*

Prayer Starter

Thank you, my Father in heaven, for caring for me as your child. Thank you for being concerned about every aspect of my life, however small. Give me the bread of serving you this day.

10

Many Ways to Pray

When they had sung the hymn, they went out to the Mount of Olives.

Mark 14:26

Human beings are creatures of habit, often unconscious habit. If we do anything repeatedly, we will begin to do it in the same way, time after time. Our prayers can also assume a familiar pattern. We may become so comfortable with this pattern that we end up thinking that it is the only way to pray or the only way we can pray. However, when we note in the Gospels how Jesus prayed, we discover that he prayed in a great variety of ways.

Most of Jesus' prayers were spontaneous prayers, appropriate to the moment. But Jesus also made full use of his Jewish heritage and prayed the psalms. At the end of the Last Supper, "when they had sung the hymn, they went out to the Mount of Olives" (Mark 14:26). This "hymn" was almost certainly Psalms 113–118, which were recited at great feasts and were used to close the Passover meal. Jesus prayed at least portions of two psalms from the cross (see Mark 15:34 and Psalm 22:1; Luke 23:46 and Psalm 31:5). Both traditional prayers and spontaneous prayers had a place in Jesus' prayer life, and they have a place in the prayer life of his followers as well.

Sometimes Jesus' prayers were prayers of praise and jubilation, as when the disciples came back victorious from their mission (see Luke 10:21). At other times his prayers were prayers of sorrow and anguish, as in Gethsemane (see Luke 22:39–46). In the same way, our prayers will sometimes be prayers of praise and rejoicing. We have many scriptural models for such prayers: the many psalms of praise (see Psalm 150, for example) or the prayers of praise found in the book of Revelation (see 5:9–14, for example). At other times our prayers will be more somber: we will come before God, asking for his forgiveness in the mood of Psalm 51; we will search our ways in the sight of God, asking for his mercy in the manner of Psalm 25.

Jesus prayed that his Father might guide him, that he might act in perfect accordance with God's will. Before Jesus chose twelve of his followers to be his special apostles, he spent a whole night in prayer (see Luke 6:12–13). Sometimes Jesus' prayer was a prayer of thanksgiving (see Luke 10:21). In the same way, our prayers should include seeking God's guidance and giving thanks for all that our Father has done for us.

Jesus also interceded for others, particularly his close followers. He turned to his Father for the power to heal the sick and raise the dead (see Mark 7:34; John 11:41). He interceded for his disciples, those his Father had given into his care, that they would be kept safe after he returned to his Father (see John 17:15). He prayed for Peter, that his faith would not fail under Satan's assaults (see Luke 22:31–32). We likewise are called to intercede for those whom we are responsible for, for our family, for our close friends. As we pray for those we love, the example of Jesus should be before us.

Prayer in Solitude

Jesus often went off by himself to pray, arising in the morning before the disciples or going to some solitary place. This setting for prayer is most conducive to reflecting on the mystery of God's plan unfolding in our lives, just as Mary pondered in her heart the events surrounding the birth of her Son, Jesus (see Luke 2:51). Jesus likewise made use of prayer in solitude to ponder his mission on earth. Thus, after Jesus heard of the death of his forerunner, John the Baptizer, he "withdrew from there in a boat to a deserted place by himself " (Matthew 14:13), presumably so that he could have the privacy to enter into prayerful communion with his Father. John's death signaled the end of a preparation stage; now Jesus wanted to be alone with his Father so that he could contemplate what lay before him.

The same type of prayer is necessary for us. Being a Christian is not a matter of obeying a certain set of rules that we can memorize and follow without need for further direction. Being a Christian primarily means entering into a personal relationship with God. Sustaining and nourishing that relationship requires personal contact with God. We must ponder in our hearts the mystery of his presence in our lives and discern his will for us. Such prayer is different from exuberant jubilation or loving intercession.

Peaceful reflection on the mysteries of our faith is necessary for our growth in faith.

Prayer with Others

Jesus taught his followers, "Whenever you pray, go into your room and shut the door and pray to your Father who is in secret; and your Father who sees in secret will reward you" (Matthew 6:6). Jesus was warning against public ostentation in prayer, but he was not teaching that our prayer should be exclusively private. Jesus himself went aside to pray, but he also prayed with the apostles and in their presence. It was because the apostles saw Jesus praying that they asked him to teach them how to pray (see Luke 11:1). During the Last Supper, Jesus led the apostles in the prayers and psalms of the Passover, adding his own words to the prayers of thanksgiving over the bread and wine (see Mark 14:26). Thus, for Jesus, prayer was to be done not only in one's closet in solitude but also with others.

Jesus chose three apostles—Peter, James, and John—to join him in special times of prayer. They were with him when he was transfigured during prayer: "Jesus took with him Peter and John and James, and went up on the mountain to pray. And while he was praying, the appearance of his face changed, and his clothes became dazzling white" (Luke 9:28–29). Jesus asked Peter and James and John to be near him during his most intense and personal prayer recorded in the Gospels: his agony in Gethsemane before his crucifixion.

> They went to a place called Gethsemane; and he said to his disciples, "Sit here while I pray." He took with him Peter and James and John, and began to be distressed and agitated. And he said to them, "I am deeply grieved, even to death; remain here, and keep awake." And going a little farther, he threw himself on the ground and prayed. (Mark 14:32–35)

The cup that Jesus had to drink was a cup that he alone could empty. Even so, Jesus' most private moment of prayer was also a moment when he wanted the support of his followers.

Our Prayer

Jesus likewise invited us to support each other in prayer. He promised his special presence when we gather in his name to pray; he promised a special power to our prayers when we come together to present our needs to his Father: "Again, truly I tell you, if two of you agree on earth about anything you ask, it will be done for you by my Father in heaven. For where two or three are gathered in my name, I am there among them" (Matthew 18:19–20).

There is therefore a communal, as well as a private, dimension to our prayer. The union between our Father and us that prayer nourishes also involves the other children of the same Father. It is fitting that we join with each other in prayer in the variety of ways that we can pray with others. Sometimes we pray as a part of a large worshiping congregation; sometimes we pray with just one other person—a spouse or close friend. Sometimes shared prayer in small groups can help us as we seek to praise our Father and grow in his life.

It is noteworthy that the prayer that Jesus taught his followers is a collective, not an individual, prayer. We do not pray, "*My* Father . . . give *me* this day *my* daily bread." We say, "*Our* Father . . . give *us* this day *our* daily bread. . . . Forgive *us our* trespasses, as *we* forgive. . . . Lead *us* not into temptation, but deliver *us* from evil." To be a son or daughter of the Father is to be a brother or sister with Jesus and with each other.

For Reflection

- *Am I more comfortable praying with others or praying alone?*
- *Do all my prayers fall into a familiar pattern?*
- *Are there any kinds of prayer that I am neglecting?*

Prayer Starter

Father, there is so much that I could say to you in prayer, but I often say so little. Give me words to praise and beseech you, to ask your forgiveness and thank you.

11

Evaluating How We Pray

Two men went up to the temple to pray, one a Pharisee and the other a tax collector. The Pharisee, standing by himself, was praying thus, "God, I thank you that I am not like other people: thieves, rogues, adulterers, or even like this tax collector. I fast twice a week; I give a tenth of all my income." But the tax collector, standing far off, would not even look up to heaven, but was beating his breast and saying, "God, be merciful to me, a sinner!" I tell you, this man went down to his home justified rather than the other; for all who exalt themselves will be humbled, but all who humble themselves will be exalted.

Luke 18:10–14

To understand the full impact of Jesus' parable, we must take the prayers of the Pharisee and the tax collector at face value. We must assume they meant what they prayed and were not simply putting on an act.

The Pharisee's Prayer

We will also miss much of the impact of the parable if we view the Pharisee with a totally unsympathetic eye. Many favorable things can be said about the Pharisees in the time of Jesus. They were zealous to obey God's laws as they understood them. In insisting on observance of the fine points of their traditions, they sometimes overlooked more important matters (don't we all?). But Pharisees were not evil men; they were religious men who were misguided in some of their zeal.

The Pharisee's prayer conveyed both true devotion and a tragic flaw. He fasted twice a week; he was scrupulous in paying tithes on all his income. He was not engaged in a disreputable occupation, like collecting taxes for Rome, a pagan power. He did not steal; he did not commit adultery. He gave thanks to God for his righteousness: he had come to the temple, after all, to pray. In contrast, a good deal of the rest of the world was unjust and adulterous, and a good many other Jews were slipshod in their observance of the law. The prayer of this Pharisee contained much truth, and the life of the Pharisee contained much that was commendable.

Yet the prayer of the Pharisee did not meet with God's favor. This Pharisee's virtue had become a source of pride; he looked down on anyone who could not live up to the code of conduct that he followed. His prayer ended up becoming, as some translations have it, "a prayer to himself," not a prayer offered humbly to God. However eloquent the words that he used, it was a prayer of self-satisfaction, of self-righteousness.

The Tax Collector's Prayer

The prayer of the tax collector was quite different. He was engaged in an occupation considered sinful, and he may have used his position to extort money (many officials did: see Luke 3:12–14). He could not come up with an impressive list of religious accomplishments. He was aware that he fell short of fulfilling the law at many points. He consequently felt very sinful and at a distance from God. He did not pray a prayer of praise or thanks to God; he could not even raise his eyes to heaven. He could only dare a humble prayer of reliance on God's mercy. He may not have thought that he was praying a very good prayer; he probably left the temple feeling that his prayer must have been insignificant in the ears of God, who was used to hearing much better prayers from much holier people.

Yet Jesus told us that it was the tax collector's prayer that found favor in God's sight!

How Do We Pray?

We can have characteristics of both the Pharisee and the tax collector. On the one hand, if we are aware of the call we have received from God, if we are aware that we are leading lives that are more virtuous than those of many in the world today, then we can fall into the Pharisee's error: subtly (or not so subtly) looking down on others because they do not follow the way of life that we do. This parable of Jesus can be a stiff reminder to us that no matter how favored we are in the sight of God and no matter how misguided and sinful the world might be, we incur God's judgment by despising others. If such an attitude infects our prayers, then our prayers are in danger of becoming prayers to ourselves: prayers of self-satisfaction, prayers of self-righteousness.

We can also find ourselves praying as the tax collector prayed: aware of how far we fall short of God's plan for us, feeling at a distance from God, unable to pray a prayer of thanksgiving or praise with any conviction. Indeed, all we can do with conviction is beg for God's mercy. We may feel that we are not very good at prayer and that the words that meander through our minds when we try to pray cannot be very impressive to God. We may wonder on some days if we should consider our prayer time to be prayer at all, since it seems to be filled from beginning to end with distractions. We may even lapse into an awkward silence in the presence of God, grasping for some words, any words, to offer in prayer.

It is reassuring that Jesus told us that the tax collector's prayer was found acceptable by God. God viewed the tax collector more favorably than the tax collector viewed himself; God evaluated his prayer much more highly than the tax collector probably evaluated it. God was pleased with the tax collector's humble offering of himself, and God honored his cry for mercy.

If the Pharisee's attitude of evaluating others is dangerous, so too there is danger in trying to evaluate ourselves too scrupulously, particularly when it comes to our prayers. We do need to examine ourselves before God and turn to him for forgiveness when we have sinned. But if we pay more attention to how we are praying than to the one we are praying to, we may end up either puffed up like the Pharisee at how well we are able to pray or dejected that our prayer was so halting and inarticulate. If we focus on our prayers too closely, we may be tempted to give up praying. Why walk to the temple every day when all we can manage when we get there is a meager, "God, be merciful to me, a sinner"? If we demand that our prayer time be rewarding every day, we may fall away from prayer in disappointment.

The lesson of the tax collector is that we may not be very good judges of how well we pray. Our Father hears our cries for mercy, no matter how unholy we feel, no matter how aware we are of our sins, no matter how distant we feel from him—for he is close by our side when we pray.

For Reflection

- *Do I believe that God is really interested in my prayers, no matter how stumbling they are?*
- *Do I believe that he loves me, despite my sins?*
- *Do I believe he hears my cries when I turn to him?*

Prayer Starter

Father, teach me to be grateful for all the good things you have given me and done for me, but without my looking down on any other person. Let me see my sins clearly, but without despairing over them. Give me a heart that is pleasing to you.

12

Facing Difficulties in Prayer

In the days of his flesh, Jesus offered up prayers and
supplications, with loud cries and tears, to the one who
was able to save him from death, and he was heard
because of his reverent submission. Although he was a
Son, he learned obedience through what he suffered.

Hebrews 5:7–8

While Jesus had trouble getting away from the
clamoring crowds in order to pray, he also
faced other difficulties in prayer. Jesus was the Son
of God, but he was also Jesus of Nazareth, the
carpenter, a man who fully shared in every aspect
of the human condition, save sin. Jesus experienced the full range of human emotions, from joy
(see Luke 10:21) to sorrow (see Luke 19:41–44;
John 11:35). In the letter to the Hebrews we read,
"We do not have a high priest who is unable to
sympathize with our weaknesses, but we have one
who in every respect has been tested as we are, yet

without sin" (4:15). Jesus Christ experienced our weaknesses; Jesus Christ was tempted as we are tempted.

Jesus' full sharing of the human condition extended even to his prayer life. The letter to the Hebrews describes Jesus offering "prayers and supplications, with loud cries and tears" (5:7). This is the description not of someone whose prayer life was one of effortless ease and endless consolation but of someone who struggled in prayer, even as we struggle.

The difficulties Jesus experienced in his prayer can be seen most clearly at the beginning and end of his public ministry.

The Temptations of Jesus

After his baptism, "Jesus, full of the Holy Spirit, returned from the Jordan and was led by the Spirit in the wilderness, where for forty days he was tempted by the devil" (Luke 4:1–2). These words juxtapose apparently contradictory ideas: Jesus was at one and the same time filled with the Spirit and tempted by the devil. Jesus was led by the Holy Spirit but led into the wilderness. We might think, from a human perspective, that being filled with the Holy Spirit should banish all temptations, or at least make a person immune to them. We might think that the Spirit would lead a person to a peaceful place of rest, not into a desert. But it was not so with Jesus—and it is not so with us.

During his stay in the desert, Jesus "fasted forty days and forty nights, and afterwards he was famished" (Matthew 4:2). Jesus became hungry just as we become hungry, just as he became tired from journeys that would tire us, just as he had to fight against fatigue when he stayed up late at night to pray. The Gospels tell us that it was after his long fast that the devil came to tempt Jesus. The temptations came when Jesus was at low ebb physically; they came when he was most humanly vulnerable.

The temptations that the devil confronted Jesus with were temptations for Jesus to step out of God's plan for him and into a different type of messiahship. The devil tempted Jesus to become a wonder-worker who used his powers for his own advantage, turning stones into bread when he was hungry, floating majestically down from the top of the temple to win the astonishment and admiration of the crowds. The devil tempted Jesus to become a political messiah, relying on worldly might, rather than being a messiah who would die for the world. Jesus rejected these temptations as contrary to his Father's will for him, and he quoted Scripture to refute them (see Luke 4:3–13).

As with Jesus, so with us. Our bodily condition affects how we pray and what temptations we face. Some of our difficulties in prayer can be traced to physical causes. If we are fatigued, our prayers may seem leaden. If we are nervous and preoccupied, we will be more prone to distractions. If we are sick or exhausted, this will be reflected in our prayer. We are not angels; the state of our body has an impact on our spirit.

The temptations we face may also be similar to Jesus' temptations. In a time of dryness or difficulty, we may be tempted to radically change our lives, just as the devil tempted Jesus to become a different kind of messiah. Our previous commitments may look less attractive; we may long to do something different in order to get out of the desert in which we find ourselves. But this is almost always a mistake. If our basic commitment is to God, it is usually unwise to change course in a time of desolation, no matter how hopeless everything may look. In the face of dryness and temptation, we need to cling more firmly than ever to God's direction and will for us. Since we may be in no condition to discern clearly any changes in God's direction for us when we are experiencing difficulties and desolation, we should normally stay on the course we are on, no matter how unattractive it may appear.

The Gospels tell us that Jesus also faced difficult times in prayer at the end of his public ministry. The difficulties came from without—his betrayal and crucifixion—but they affected his prayer. If our prayers are more than mere words, if they express our whole life and commitment, then there is no easy line to draw between our difficulties in prayer and our difficulties in general. There was certainly no such easy line in Jesus' life.

The Agony in the Garden

After the Last Supper, Jesus went to a garden at the Mount of Olives to pray. Telling his followers to keep watch, he took Peter and James and John with him into the garden "and began to be distressed and agitated. And he said to them, 'I am deeply grieved, even to death'" (Mark 14:33–34). The trial that Jesus knew lay before him aroused in him the normal human reactions of distress and anxiety, and this was reflected in his prayer: "In his anguish he prayed more earnestly, and his sweat became like great drops of blood falling down on the ground" (Luke 22:44).

It is noteworthy that even in his agony, the prayer of Jesus was a prayer to his Father: "He threw himself on the ground and prayed that, if it were possible, the hour might pass from him. He said, 'Abba, Father, for you all things are possible; remove this cup from me; yet, not what I want, but what you want'" (Mark 14:35–36). The only passage in the Gospels that preserves for us the intimate term *Abba,* which Jesus used to address his Father, is the account of his agonized prayer in the face of death! If there was ever a moment for Jesus to feel abandoned by God, it was during those final hours. But at the time of his worst distress, Jesus prayed to his Father with the greatest intimacy and trust and love.

That intimacy is the key to our facing difficulties in our prayer, to our overcoming temptation, to our enduring times of distress, to our persevering in the face of distractions. We are praying to our Abba, to our Father. Prayer is not a matter of techniques, so that if we only knew a few more tricks we could eliminate all difficulties and dryness. Prayer is turning to our heavenly Father. Our strength in prayer, despite our problems, comes from our confidence that God is indeed our Father and loves us with a Father's love, as Jesus taught us.

Prayer from the Cross

Jesus prayed from the cross, "My God, my God, why have you forsaken me?" (Matthew 27:46). These are the opening words of Psalm 22, a psalm that ends with a confident proclamation of God's victory. But prayed from the cross, they were also a cry of distress. Jesus' anguish was real anguish, and his prayers expressed this anguish. Yet Jesus preserved his intimate relationship with his Father even from the cross: "Father, forgive them; for they do not know what they are doing" (Luke 23:34). His prayer for forgiveness for those who were putting him to death was a prayer relying on the Father's love. And at the moment of his death he prayed, "Father, into your hands I commend my spirit" (Luke 23:46). His final prayer was a prayer of confidence in his Father, an ultimate entrusting of himself into his Father's hands.

As we experience difficulties in prayer, the truth that we must cling to is Jesus' revelation of

God as our Father. The prayer we must persevere in, even if our prayer is as dry as the Judean desert, is our crying out, "Abba, Father!" The focus we must preserve, no matter what trials afflict us from within and without, is our focus on God as our loving Father. In the throes of fear and distress and doubt and anguish, we must pray, "Father." In the face of death itself, we can pray with confidence, "Father." Despite all we do not understand, despite confusions and temptations, despite whatever afflicts us, we must rely on God as our Father. That was the prayer of Jesus in the midst of his agony; that must be our prayer.

In the extremes of our difficulties, we may be tempted to believe that we have been abandoned by God—perhaps because of our sins, perhaps simply because of some oversight on God's part. We may no longer experience his presence in the way we once did. We may no longer be able to pray as we once were able to. We may be tempted to doubt that God is really our Father.

This is a temptation that we must meet head-on. If we are tempted to believe that God has abandoned us, the solution is to abandon ourselves into his hands. Jesus prayed in his time of agony, "Not my will but yours be done" (Luke 22:42). That is also the prayer that Jesus taught us to pray: "Our Father . . . your will be done" (Matthew 6:9, 10). Jesus' prayer in Gethsemane is echoed by us every time we pray the Our Father. In a time of trial, every follower of Jesus must likewise echo his prayer from the cross, "Father, into your hands I commend my spirit" (Luke 23:46). Thus did Stephen, the first martyr, at the point of his death: "Lord Jesus, receive my spirit" (Acts 7:59). Our prayer of abandoning ourselves into the hands of our Father—"your will be done"—is our ultimate response in the face of difficulties, just as it was the ultimate response of Jesus.

For Reflection

- *What is the greatest temptation or difficulty I am facing right now?*
- *Am I able to pray to God as my Father and say, "Your will be done"?*

Prayer Starter

Abba, Father, I place myself in your hands. I put all my hope in your love for me. May your will be done in my life.

13

Praying in the Spirit

I am sending upon you what my Father promised; so stay here in the city until you have been clothed with power from on high.

Luke 24:49

Jesus came to bring us the Holy Spirit. He came to show us the way to his Father—and that way is the way of the Spirit. He came to bring us abundant life—and that life is the life of the Spirit. He came to teach us to pray as he prayed—and that is prayer in the Spirit.

If Jesus constantly lived in relationship to the Father, he also lived in the fullness of the Holy Spirit. The beginning of Jesus' public ministry was marked by his baptism by John, and while he was at prayer after his baptism, "the Holy Spirit descended upon him in bodily form like a dove. And a voice came from heaven, 'You are my Son, the Beloved; with you I am well pleased'" (Luke 3:22). This event inaugurated Jesus' mission on earth, and it manifested both his sonship to the Father and the presence of the Holy Spirit within him.

The Holy Spirit and Jesus

The Spirit was never absent from Jesus' life. The Gospels give us many glimpses of how Jesus was "full of the Holy Spirit" (Luke 4:1). When Jesus rejoiced that the Father had revealed himself to his followers, he "rejoiced in the Holy Spirit" (Luke 10:21). When Jesus instructed his followers, it was "through the Holy Spirit" (Acts 1:2). Jesus did the works of the Father in the power of the Spirit; he prayed to his Father through the Spirit; he was guided in his Father's will by the Spirit.

Jesus promised the same Holy Spirit to his followers. He stood up on the last day of the Feast of Tabernacles in Jerusalem and cried out, "Let anyone who is thirsty come to me, and let the one who believes in me drink" (John 7:37–38). John explains that Jesus was referring to the living water that he would give, that is, the Holy Spirit, who would be poured out on those who believed in Jesus after he was glorified (see John 7:39).

According to John's Gospel, Jesus instructed his followers about the Holy Spirit during the Last Supper. Jesus described the Holy Spirit as an advocate—one who would teach and guide, protect and help his followers, just as Jesus himself had done during his years on earth. "I will ask the Father, and he will give you another Advocate, to be with you forever" (John 14:16). The Advocate would be the "Spirit of truth" (John 14:17) and would carry on the mission of Jesus:

> Whoever does not love me does not keep my words; and the word that you hear is not mine, but is from the Father who sent me. I have said these things to you while I am still with you. But the Advocate, the Holy Spirit, whom the Father will send in my name, will teach you everything, and remind you of all that I have said to you. (John 14:24–26)

Just as Jesus did not proclaim his own message but taught the message given to him by his Father, so the Holy Spirit continues to bring the Father's message to humanity. The Holy Spirit "will not speak on his own, but will speak whatever he hears, and he will declare to you the things that are to come" (John 16:13). The Holy Spirit carries on the work of Jesus, which was to carry out the mission of his Father. There is thus such a unity within the Trinity that we can say equally well that Jesus came to show us the way to his Father and that Jesus came to bring us the Holy Spirit.

Jesus told his followers that it was to their advantage that he leave them: "For if I do not go away, the Advocate will not come to you; but if I go, I will send him to you" (John 16:7). After his resurrection, he told his followers to remain in Jerusalem: "I am sending upon you what my Father promised; so stay here in the city until you have been clothed with power from on high" (Luke 24:49). Jesus made his meaning explicit before ascending to heaven: "You will be baptized with the Holy Spirit not many days from now" (Acts 1:5). Once the followers of Jesus received the power of the Holy Spirit, they could be his witnesses in Jerusalem and Judea and even to the ends of the earth (see Acts 1:8).

Jesus Sends His Spirit

When the Holy Spirit came on those gathered in prayer in the upper room on Pentecost, they received him and began to proclaim the good news about Jesus Christ boldly and powerfully. They were transformed from a small group who hid in fear behind locked doors (see John 20:19) to a rapidly growing church that added three thousand members to its number in the wake of the Spirit's coming on Pentecost. The pages of the Acts of the Apostles are a chronicle of the power of the Holy Spirit and his presence in the early church.

Jesus promised the Holy Spirit to all who believe in him. Peter told those who gathered in amazement on the day of Pentecost that they too could receive the Holy Spirit in the same way that the apostles had: "For the promise is for you, for your children, and for all who are far away, everyone whom the Lord our God calls to him" (Acts 2:39). Jesus had previously taught that the Father would send the Holy Spirit on those who asked in prayer to receive him: "If you then, who are evil, know how to give good gifts to your children, how much more will the heavenly Father give the Holy Spirit to those who ask him!" (Luke 11:13).

When the Holy Spirit comes into our lives, he makes us adopted children of the Father. "Because you are children, God has sent the Spirit of his Son into our hearts, crying, 'Abba! Father!' So you are no longer a slave but a child, and if a child then also an heir, through God" (Galatians 4:6–7). We become sons and daughters of our heavenly Father through the presence of the Spirit within us. Jesus' mission to bring us the Holy Spirit was the same as his mission to provide us access to his Father.

There is also an inextricable link between the presence of the Spirit within us and the ability to pray to God as our Father. Jesus could authorize us to pray to God as our Father because he was providing for our adoption as sons and daughters through his Holy Spirit.

> For all who are led by the Spirit of God are children of God. For you did not receive a spirit of slavery to fall back into fear, but you have received a spirit of adoption. When we cry, "Abba! Father!" it is that very Spirit bearing witness with our spirit that we are children of God. (Romans 8:14–16)

The Spirit Prays in Us

The Holy Spirit also gives us the guidance and strength to pray to God as our Father:

The Spirit helps us in our weakness; for we do not know how to pray as we ought, but that very Spirit intercedes with sighs too deep for words. And God, who searches the heart, knows what is the mind of the Spirit, because the Spirit intercedes for the saints according to the will of God. (Romans 8:26–27)

Paul is referring here to the general guidance that the Spirit gives us in our prayers—and probably also making reference to the Spirit's gift of praying in tongues, a gift that Paul discusses at length in his first letter to the Corinthians (see chapters 12–14). We need the presence of the Spirit to pray, "Abba, Father"; we need the inspiration of the Spirit to know how to pray as we ought; we need the gift of the Spirit to pray in a way that expresses the love of our hearts.

The human condition is one of weakness, and nowhere is this more apparent than in our prayers. Those who have attempted prayer for any period of time know from experience how weak our powers of prayer are, how easily we are distracted, how heavy our hearts and words are on some days. It is clear that we need a power beyond our own to pray with ease, with joy, with endurance. We need an ability beyond our own to truly offer words of fitting praise to God. We need faith beyond our own to pray for healing for those we love. We need the joy of the Spirit to lift our hearts when they are heavy. We need to pray for the Holy Spirit to be ever more present in our lives so that we may pray with the power of the Spirit. It is only in the Spirit that we are able to pray to God as our Father, as our Abba. It is in the Spirit that we are able to pray as Jesus prayed.

For Reflection

- *Has the Holy Spirit helped me to pray?*
- *Have I ever asked for his help?*

Prayer Starter

Come, Holy Spirit, fill my heart and mind. Give me words of prayer, that I may speak with my God and Father.

14

Learning from the Longest Prayer

Father, the hour has come; glorify your Son so that the Son may glorify you.

John 17:1

J esus speaks in a majestic voice in the Gospel of John. It is as if the author of this Gospel has meditated for many years on the risen and glorified Jesus and is able to convey some of Jesus' risen glory, even as he writes about the public ministry of Jesus. John's Gospel also contains the longest prayer in the New Testament: Jesus' prayer during the Last Supper makes up all of chapter 17. As we might expect, this prayer has lessons for what our own prayers should be like.

The context of the prayer is important: Jesus has just finished the last meal he will share with his friends and followers before his death. He has given them his final instructions, his new law of love. He has given them the new covenant of his body and blood. And now he concludes their time together with prayer.

As with every prayer of Jesus, this prayer is addressed to his Father. In the twenty-six verses that make up this chapter of John's Gospel, Jesus refers to himself more than fifty times and likewise addresses or refers to his Father more than fifty times. Every verse averages five references by Jesus to himself or his Father: "*Father,* the hour has come; glorify *your Son* so that the *Son* may glorify *you,* since *you* have given *him* authority over all people, to give eternal life to all whom *you* have given *him*" (John 17:1–2, italics added).

Personal Prayer

This prayer of Jesus to his Father is hence not an abstract, all-purpose prayer giving praise to a distant God. It is the prayer of the Son addressed to his Father in personal terms. It is a prayer built around the words *I* and *you.* It is one person talking to another person, as an expression of their intimate relationship.

Along with being a very personal prayer, it is also a very reverential prayer. Jesus prays in an intimate way to his Father, but in a way that is also deeply respectful. Jesus offers profound worship to his Father as God, yet he talks in an intimate way to God as his Father.

Nor is Jesus' prayer a self-centered prayer, despite its constant use of the words *I* and *me*. The focus of the prayer is the Father. Jesus often refers to himself, but characteristically in terms of his relationship with his Father. Jesus mentions the power over mankind that he has, but he acknowledges that this power is given to him by the Father (see John 17:2). The work Jesus did on earth was the work given to him by his Father; the followers of Jesus were those who were given to him by the Father. Indeed, everything that Jesus has and does comes from the Father because all that Jesus has is the Father's and all that the Father has belongs to Jesus (see John 17:10).

In this prayer Jesus does not merely offer prayer to his Father; he offers himself. His prayer is a summary of his life and mission, prayed on the eve of his death. "Father, the hour has come" (John 17:1). Jesus is near the end of the mission given to him by his Father; now he offers himself up as his final act. Jesus reaffirms that he is in the Father's hands and offers his life for God's glory.

This prayer of Jesus is hence a prayer of praise. Jesus prays for himself, but so that the Father may be glorified: "Glorify your Son so that the Son may glorify you" (John 17:1). Just as the whole life of Jesus was spent carrying out the work of the Father, to his glory, so this concluding prayer is offered for the glory of God.

Jesus' prayer is also a prayer of intercession. He prays for his friends and followers, as those that the Father had given into his care. In his poverty Jesus does not even claim his followers as his own but acknowledges that they were selected and sent to him by his Father. Jesus made the Father known to them; he taught them in accordance with the Father's plan; he passed on the word of God to them; he watched over them and cared for them. Now the time has come to send them into the world, just as the Father sent Jesus into the world. Jesus therefore does not pray that his followers be removed from the world but that they be protected from the evil one, that is, the devil (see John 17:15). As his final act of love for his followers before his death, Jesus prays for his Father's protection upon them in the days ahead, when he will no longer be able to walk by their side as he had in the past.

Jesus concludes by praying for the unity of his followers—not only the unity of those at the Last Supper, but also the unity of all who would believe in him through the apostles' preaching. Jesus prays that the unity of his followers may be so great and so obvious that it will be an effective sign of his divine sonship: "that they may become completely one, so that the world may know that you have sent me and have loved them even as you have loved me" (John 17:23).

Five Aspects

Many elements from Jesus' prayer during the Last Supper can serve as a model for us when we pray. In particular, five aspects of this prayer may guide us as we enter into prayer to the Father: Jesus' identity as the Son, Jesus' reverence and praise, Jesus' offering of himself to the Father, Jesus' intercession for those he was responsible for, and Jesus' prayer for unity.

1. Jesus' prayer is based upon his identity as the Son of God. Our prayer likewise must be based upon our identity as children of God. Our prayer should be an expression of the relationship that Jesus established between his Father and us. We do not turn to God in prayer as mere

men and women seeking God; we turn to our Father as his adopted sons and daughters, with simplicity and trust.

2. At the same time, our prayer should be marked by the reverence and praise that characterizes the Last Supper prayer of Jesus. Our Father is God; we have been created by him as well as adopted by him. God deserves reverence and awe, praise and adoration.

3. Jesus' prayer in conclusion of the Last Supper is also a prayer in conclusion of his years on earth. It is a prayer in which Jesus offers up his whole life and mission to his Father and places himself in his Father's hands. Our prayer should also strive toward this fundamental self-giving. Prayer is not a matter of offering mere words to God but a matter of offering ourselves.

4. Jesus intercedes for those whom he was responsible for. We too should take a special concern in prayer for those in our care and those we care about: our family and friends, those whom we are joined with in Christian fellowship. We should intercede every day for them, taking their concerns before God as our concerns, praying for their well-being and divine protection.

5. Jesus prays for the unity of his followers. His concern for unity should also be in our hearts. We should pray that those who acknowledge the same Lord will be one in heart and mind with each other; we should pray that those who call upon the same God as their Father will be joined as his *children with each other.*

For Reflection

Read chapter 17 of John's Gospel slowly, paying particular attention to how Jesus speaks of himself in relation to his Father.

- *What does this chapter tell me about Jesus, his Father, and their relationship?*

Prayer Starter

Father, I offer you my life; I give you my very self. All I have comes from you; all that I am I place before you.

15

The Breaking of the Bread

While they were eating, Jesus took a loaf of bread, and after blessing it he broke it, gave it to the disciples, and said, "Take, eat; this is my body." Then he took a cup, and after giving thanks he gave it to them, saying, "Drink from it, all of you; for this is my blood of the covenant, which is poured out for many for the forgiveness of sins."

Matthew 26:26–28

J esus' words and actions during the Last Supper were astounding. Bread and wine were standard fare at Jewish ceremonial meals like Passover. But for anyone to pass bread, saying, "Take, eat; this is my body," and to pass a cup of wine and say, "Drink from it, all of you, for this is my blood," and to add that sins will be forgiven through an outpouring of his blood— that is so astounding that either we must think him crazed or we must bow down before him in awe and adoration. There doesn't seem to be any comfortable middle ground: we can't give our allegiance to Jesus as simply a teacher of profound truths when he gave us bread and wine as his body and blood. Either he was out of his mind (see Mark 3:21) or he had authority and power to do what no human being can do: forgive sins (see Mark 2:5–11) and give his body to be eaten and his blood to be drunk.

There is little in the Gospels of Matthew, Mark, and Luke to prepare the reader for the astounding words and actions of Jesus during the Last Supper. John's Gospel, however, presents us with a discourse of Jesus that proclaims his flesh to be our food and his blood our drink, as nourishment that brings us eternal life.

The Living Bread

Jesus' words in the Gospel of John are as bold as his words during the Last Supper: "I am the living bread that came down from heaven. Whoever eats of this bread will live forever; and the bread that I will give for the life of the world is my flesh" (John 6:51). Jesus' claims are earthshaking: that he is not merely from earth like us but also from heaven, that he will give us his flesh to eat, that those who eat his flesh will not be held by death but will have eternal life, that his gift of himself as bread will bring life to the entire world.

Those who first heard this claim were startled by it. They asked one another, "How can this man give us his flesh to eat?" (John 6:52). Had they heard Jesus wrong? Jesus immediately answered them to clear up any misunderstanding:

> Very truly, I tell you, unless you eat the flesh of the Son of Man and drink his blood, you have no life in you. Those who eat my flesh and drink my blood have eternal life, and I will raise them up on the last day; for my flesh is true food and my blood is true drink. (John 6:53–55)

The crowd was shocked. In their eyes Jesus was only "the son of Joseph, whose father and mother we know" (John 6:42). Even those who considered themselves his followers said, "This teaching is difficult; who can accept it?" (John 6:60). And "because of this many of his disciples turned back and no longer went about with him" (John 6:66).

We, too, should be awestruck by these claims. If we are not, then perhaps they have become too familiar to us. We should not try to make faith more difficult. But if our faith can rest easy with such radical claims of Jesus, then either we should be concerned that the message of the gospel has become commonplace for us or we should be very grateful that a great gift of faith has been given to us.

Jesus did not seem surprised that many of his followers left him. To truly believe in him and follow him required a gift of faith from his Father: "For this reason I have told you that no one can come to me unless it is granted by the Father" (John 6:65).

Jesus himself even questioned the faith of the twelve apostles: "'Do you also wish to go away?' Simon Peter answered him, 'Lord, to whom can we go? You have the words of eternal life'" (John 6:67–68). We are in Peter's shoes: to whom could we go in hope of receiving eternal life, save to Jesus?

In Memory of Jesus

During the Last Supper, Jesus celebrated the memory of the old covenant in the Passover meal and transformed it into a celebration of the new covenant that he was establishing between his Father and his followers. Jesus took the bread and wine of the old covenant and gave them to his followers as his body and blood, as the basis of the new covenant. And he commanded them, "Do this in remembrance of me" (Luke 22:19).

This blessing and breaking of bread as the body of Christ became an integral part of the life of the early church. When the early Christians gathered together to pray, they did not merely offer words of prayer; they offered the body and blood of Jesus Christ. Their prayer was not only a matter of what they said but also a matter of what they did. And what they did, they did in imitation of what Jesus did during the Last Supper, in obedience to his command. When Luke wished to summarize the life of the Jerusalem church, he characterized the followers of Jesus as devoting themselves "to the apostles' teaching and fellowship, to the breaking of bread and the prayers" (Acts 2:42). When Paul wished to instruct the church at Corinth in the proper way to worship God together, he wrote:

> For I received from the Lord what I also handed on to you, that the Lord Jesus on the night when he was betrayed took a loaf of bread, and when he had given thanks, he broke it and said, "This

is my body that is for you. Do this in remembrance of me." In the same way he took the cup also, after supper, saying, "This cup is the new covenant in my blood. Do this, as often as you drink it, in remembrance of me." For as often as you eat this bread and drink the cup, you proclaim the Lord's death until he comes. Whoever, therefore, eats the bread or drinks the cup of the Lord in an unworthy manner will be answerable for the body and blood of the Lord. (1 Corinthians 11:23–27)

Sharing in Christ's Body and Blood

When Christians gathered in prayer, they did not merely share fellowship with one another; they shared in the blood of Christ. Their unity with one another was not merely a unity of common belief; it was a unity of the body of Christ: "The cup of blessing that we bless, is it not a sharing in the blood of Christ? The bread that we break, is it not a sharing in the body of Christ? Because there is one bread, we who are many are one body, for we all partake of the one bread" (1 Corinthians 10:16–17).

Sharing in the body and blood of Christ was integral to Christian fellowship and worship. Luke describes Paul's visit to the city of Troas:

"On the first day of the week, . . . we met to break bread" (Acts 20:7). In the breaking of the bread, Jesus became present to them, just as he manifested himself to the two disciples on the road to Emmaus in the breaking of the bread (see Luke 24:28–35).

Jesus gave us access to his Father in prayer. Jesus also gave us himself, completely and totally. He gave himself throughout his life; he gave himself on Calvary; he gave himself as the living bread. His church still celebrates his real presence in its midst. His church still offers the body and blood of Christ in prayer to the Father, sharing in this offering of eternal life.

For Reflection

- *Do I have awe for Jesus' gift of his body and blood to me in the Eucharist?*
- *How do I express my awe and reverence for this gift?*

Prayer Starter

Thank you, Lord Jesus Christ, for giving your very self to me in the Eucharist. Thank you for the gift of eternal life.

16

"When You Pray, Say: Father"

He said to them, "When you pray, say:
  Father, hallowed be your name.
    Your kingdom come.
    Give us each day our daily bread.
    And forgive us our sins,
      for we ourselves forgive everyone indebted to us.
    And do not bring us to the time of trial."

Luke 11:2–4

J esus' prayers were unique because they were prayers to God as his Father. As such, they were at the heart of his identity and mission. Jesus came among us as the Son of God, and he prayed to God as a son speaks to his father.

Our prayers are also at the heart of our identity as Christians. Because Jesus lived among us as the Son of God and died for us, we can become sons and daughters of God. Through the presence of the Spirit of Jesus Christ within us, we can be adopted as children of God. Jesus authorized those who found life in him to pray to his Father as their Father.

Therefore, we can turn to God in prayer and call upon him as our Father. Because of Jesus, we can do what none of us could dare do on our own: address the creator of the universe personally, intimately, directly. We still need to acknowledge that God is God and we are his creatures; we still need to acknowledge the holiness of God and his authority over us. But we do not need to approach God in fear; we can approach him with the confidence of sons and daughters. We can come before God for our needs; we can even ask him for our daily bread.

Our prayer to God as our Father is not a secondary feature of our lives as Christians. It reflects the basic nature of our redemption: we have been made children of God through the death and resurrection of Jesus Christ and the presence of the Holy Spirit within us. Our prayer is an expression of our status as sons and daughters of God. Our prayer is conversation with our Father in heaven.

Jesus Christ lived among us as the Son of God so that we might become adopted children of God. He prayed to his Father as a Son and taught us to pray as sons and daughters. He taught us to pray as he prayed.

For Reflection

- *What does being a child of God mean for me?*
- *How do my prayers express my being a child of God?*

Prayer Starter

Thank you, my Father in heaven, for creating me and making me your child. Thank you for sending your Son, Jesus, so that I might receive the Holy Spirit. Thank you for inviting me to be with you for all eternity.